LEADERSHIP MATTERS:
LEADERS BORN
OR MADE?

LEADERSHIP MODELS

DR. SABELO SAM GASELA MHLANGA

INDEPENDENTLY PUBLISHED BY:
DR. SABELO SAM GASELA MHLANGA

ISBN: 979-8-9899221-2-3

CONTENTS

PREFACE

Leadership is the most fundamental vehicle that drives family, churches, societies, organizations, companies, nationals, and the entire world. The political, religious, business, and civil society leadership plays a pivotal role to drive political, economic, spiritual, and civil society in a given entity. However, leaders can have a positive influence to build up the entity or a negative influence that can bring down and destroy the entity. Choosing and electing leaders requires soberness, intelligence, discernment, and aptitude. The qualities, character, lifestyle, and attitude of a leader are a window to see whether the entity will succeed or fall, all rest on the leadership. The rhetorical question, are the leaders born or made, is the fundamental question that will be explored in this book. This question has not been adequately answered whether leaders are born or made. The book attempts to explore and discuss leaders in the political-religious and civil society in order to determine if that rhetorical question could be answered. The book does not give a precise answer to the rhetorical question but it is open-ended research that needs to be explored further.

I, therefore, dedicate this book to my grandfather, Mabutho Gasela, my father, Joseph Gasela, and my mother Josephine Gasela for their leadership in our family, to my wife Judith Gasela and our five children, Qhawe Blessing, Sinqobile Shalom, Thandolwenkosi Prosper, Nkosilathi Emmanuel, Joseph Sam Nkosana, my brothers, Ernest, Alexander, Joshua, Adwell, Zenzo and Sipho. Rev. Jealous Manyumbu who was my incredible Pastor during my High School, Dr. Bishop Joshua Dhube, who was my

Church Chairman and I was his Vice Church Chairman of United Baptist Church. I also dedicate this book to Dr. Joshua Mqabuko Nkomo, the President of PF-ZAPU and ZIPRA, and the Vice President of Zimbabwe. I also dedicate this book to two of my friend, James Cornwell and John Makiya from Multicare Health System whom I worked with so well as Clinical and Spiritual Care Professionals at Tacoma General Hospital, Washington. To all my friends and family that I did not mention in this book but they have had a great impact in my life, I say I am indebted to you all.

INTRODUCTION

The quest for the truth to determine if leaders are born or made has generated the desire and enthusiasm from political, religious, business, and civil societies sectors to establish the truth whether this rhetorical question is credible or can be substantiated with facts and reality. The book explores and attempts to discuss the types of leadership, the styles of leadership, the political, biblical, civil society leadership, and kings who have had great positive or negative impacts and influences in their respective sectors.

The types of leadership such as participatory, autocratic, authoritative, and democratic are discussed. The styles of leadership, leader-centered leadership, people-centered or open-ended leaderships are explored. The godly and ungodly leaders and kings are discussed, extensively to determine what categories each fall. Many people are still puzzled and do not really understand the differences between born leaders and made leaders. Some people can determine between a born leader and the made leader while others do not see the differences and they cannot categorically, make a distinction. The political, religious, business, and civil societies have produced their own leaders that have influenced the whole world. Those individual leaders and kings who have influenced and impacted the world are featured in this book, whether positive or negative. There are leaders who are born with their natural abilities to influence, lead and inspire others with their natural traits and become successful. There are some leaders who are made through leadership development, mentorship and impart skills.

Some of the leaders and kings that are featured in the book are Abraham Lincoln, Nelson Mandela, Mahatma Gandi, Martin Luther King, Jr., Adolf Hitler, Idi Amin, Mao Ze Dong, Jozef Stalin, Joseph Barnabas, William Carey, Billy Graham, and King Jesus Christ. These are all very interesting leaders and, kings with their different characters and characteristics. Each leader's character and influence whether positive or negative are explored and laser-focused to give the audience the platform to examine, assess and evaluate if they are portrayed as born leaders or made leaders.

The final chapter will discuss the best and the ultimate Leader and King in the entire world, i.e., Jesus Christ as the ultimate Prophet, Priest, and King, all embedded in the incarnation, Christ, who embodies in the flesh as God-Man. Christ stands out as the best Leader and King in the entire world with the character and characteristics of a fully man and fully divine who embodied the three offices as the Prophet, the Priest, and the King of the entire universe. His leadership styles were unique and perfect, portraying both a perfect man, without sin, and divine. This is the ultimate Leader and King that the whole world needs and should learn from Him as a prototype and as a good example of a complete leader.

CHAPTER ONE
ARE LEADERS BORN OR MADE?

L eadership matters! Families, churches, organizations, companies, nations, and the world thrive or fall because of leadership. The leader is the head engine, of the family, the church, the organization, the nation to navigate, guide, lead, encourage, rebuke, counsel, console, comfort, and inspire followers. The verbs and their actions are continuous in leadership, they never end because of the nature of the position. Leadership is a process of social influence with the aim of achieving set goals and objectives that are specific, measurable, achievable, realistic, and timely (SMART). Leaders drive their followers to achieve their goals without which, the family, the church, the business, the organization, or the nation will fail. Leaders set directions, enhance inspiring visions, and have the art and skills of motivating people and influencing behaviors. Leadership requires the leader to set methods to provide directions, implementation plans, and mentoring on the way. "How leaders mobilize others to want to get extraordinary things done. It is about the practices leaders use to transform values into action, visions into realities, obstacles into innovations, separateness into solidarity, and risks into rewards."[1] Basically, leadership is taking the group of people who are willing to follow and then leading them to a certain destination, who would have caught the vision. Leadership requires the leader to make strategic plans for the organization to succeed and to achieve its goals and objectives. "Strategic planning is an organization's process of defining its strategy, or direction, and making decisions on allocating its resources to pursue this strategy, including its capital and people "[2] It is defined also as "Structured, informed, and participative process that results in decisions and actions which position an entire organization to work together at the institutional, unit (or departmental), and program levels toward a desired end state."[3]

Path-goal theory is about how leaders motivate their subordinates to accomplish designated goals. This theory is a result of research on the things that motivate employees. Other theories are in contrary to path-goal theory, for example, the situational approach which suggests that leaders must adapt to the development level of employees, contingency theory which emphasizes the match between the leader's style and specific situational variables. In contrast, the path-goal theory emphasizes the relationship between the leader's style and the characteristics of the subordinates and the work setting. This theory is based on expectancy theory which suggests that the employees will be motivated if they believe in themselves that they are able and capable of performing to the best of their abilities which would result in good outcome.

To begin with, let us examine one of the most common and popular leadership theories in the field of leadership, "Path-goal theory". The theory alludes that each organization should use the best style that can meet the subordinates' motivational needs. Leaders provide some incentives and rewards to enhance the subordinates' needs to reach their goals. Leaders motivate their employees in the path to the goals through couching and directing. Anthony and Estep cite Frederick Herzberg's theory which sums up the motivation of employees:

---

[1] James M. Kouzes and Barry Z. Posner, *Leadership Challenge 3rd.* (San-Francisco, Jossey-Bass Publishers, 2003), XVII.

[2] Strategic Planning, Retrieved on August 15, 2020, from *en.wikipedia.org|wiki*

[3] Joann Horton, Retrieved on 16 August 2011 from *cetl.matcmadison.edu|efgb|glossary.htm*

This model is referred to as the two-factor or hygiene theory. a) **Hygiene Factors**- The primary causes of unhappiness in the work environment which relate to job. When these are not provided, the employee will become dissatisfied. When appropriately provided, they will increase satisfaction. These factors include: salary, job security, working conditions, status, company policies, quality of technical supervision and quality of interpersonal relationships. b) **Motivational Factors –** The primary causes of job satisfaction. The deal directly with the content of the job itself and relate to the real nature of work that people perform. When an employee neglects to provide these factors, the staff member will experience no job satisfaction. If the employee provides a sufficient quantity of these, they will provide high job satisfaction and productivity. These factors include: achievement, recognition, responsibility, advancement, the work itself and possibility of growth. In Herzberg's hygiene factors rest on the shoulders of the administration.[4]

In brief, "Path-Goal Theory is designed to explain how leaders can help subordinates along the path to their goals by selecting specific behaviors that are best suited to subordinates' needs and actions in which subordinates are working."[5] The leadership of any organization has a mandate and a responsibility to devise ways and means if good results are anticipated.

Subordinate Characteristics show how a leader's behavior will be interpreted by subordinates in a given context. It focuses on subordinates' needs for affiliation, preferences for structure, desire for control and self-perceived level of task ability. The characteristics determine the degree subordinates find the behavior of a leader an immediate source of satisfaction or future satisfaction. Path-goal theory shows that subordinates who have strong needs for affiliation prefer supportive leadership because friendly and concerned leadership is a source of satisfaction. Those subordinates who are dogmatic and authoritarian, path-goal theory suggest that a directive leadership will be suited for such kind because it provides psychological structure and task clarity. Subordinates with internal locus

---

[4] Anthony Michael and Estep James, *Management Essentials for Christian Ministries*, Tennessee: B & H Publishers Group, 2005, 266.

[5] Peter G. Northouse, *Leadership: Practice and Theory*, London: Sage Publications, 2005, 89.

of control believe that they are in charge of the things that occur in their lives, while individuals with external locus of control believe that chance, fate, or outside forces are the determinants of life events. Path-goal theory suggests that subordinates with internal locus of control need participatory leadership because it allows subordinates to feel in charge of their work. The subordinates' perception of their own ability to perform may affect motivation.

Task characteristics have a major impact on the way a leader's behavior influences the motivation of subordinates. It includes the design of the subordinate's task, the formal authority system of the organization, and the primary work group of subordinates. A special focus of path-goal theory is on helping subordinates to over obstacles. Obstacles create excessive uncertainties, frustration or threats for subordinates. Leaders are therefore, responsible to help subordinates by removing these obstacles or helping them to overcome them.

Critic of Path-Goal Theory

Strengths

The theory is theoretically complex because it provides a set of assumptions about various leadership styles interaction with characteristics of subordinates which affect the motivation. Practically, the theory provides direction about how leaders can help subordinates to accomplish their assigned work satisfactory. The theory suggests that leaders are to choose the best leadership style that best fit the needs of subordinates and their work. Pragmatically, path-goal theory is straightforward. It provides a useful theoretical framework for understanding how various leadership behaviors affect the satisfactory and goal-directed activity of subordinates such as directives, achievement-oriented and participative. It was one of the first situational/contingency theories of leadership to explain how task and subordinate characteristics affect the impact of leadership on subordinate performance. The framework informs leaders as to how to choose an appropriate leadership based on the various demands of the task. It integrates the motivation principles of expectancy theory into a theory of leadership. It also provides a model that is practical. It accounts for the leaders to clarify the paths to the goals and remove or help subordinates to overcome the obstacles. It reminds leadership to guide and coach subordinates as they aim at achieving set goals.

Weaknesses

Path-goal theory is so complex and incorporates so many different aspects of leadership that interpreting the meaning of the theory can be confusing. The theory on styles does not adequately show how leaders' styles are associates with performance outcomes. Researchers have not been able to establish a consistent link between task and relationship behaviors and outcomes such as moral, job satisfaction and productivity. The other weakness is that this approach fails to find a universal style of leadership that could be effective in almost every situation. The approach was unable to identify the definitive personal characteristics of leaders and is unable to identify the universal behaviors that are associated with effective leadership.

The criticism of this theory is also that it implies that it is a daunting task to incorporate all of the factors into one's selection of a preferred leadership style. The scope of the path-goal theory is so broad and encompasses different interrelated sets of assumptions; it is difficult to utilize this theory fully. The theory has also received partial support from many empirical research studies conducted to test its validity. Path-goal theory fails to explain adequately the relationship between leadership behavior and worker motivation. It is a unique theory but its criticism is that it does not go enough in explicating how leadership is related to these tenets. The principle of expectancy theory suggests that subordinates will be motivated if they feel competent and trust that their efforts will get results but it does not describe how a leader could employ various styles directly to assist subordinates to feel competent or assured of their success. It does not explain how directive leadership during ambiguous tasks increases subordinate motivation. It also does not explain how supportive leadership during tedious work relates to subordinate motivation. The practitioner is left with an inadequate understanding of how his/her leadership will affect subordinates' expectations.

In terms of practical outcome, path-goal theory, suggests that it is important for leaders to provide coaching, guidance and direction for subordinates to help them to define and clarify goals and to help subordinates around obstacles. This approach treats leadership as a one-way event and the leader affects the subordinates. The weakness in this approach is that subordinates may easily become dependent on the leader to accomplish their work. Path-goal theory puts more responsibility on leaders and less on subordinates. It can be a counterproductive style of leadership because it promotes dependency and fails to recognize the full abilities of subordinates.

Application of path-goal theory biblically and functionally

Path-goal theory provides general recommendations based on the characteristics of subordinates and tasks for how leaders should act in various situations if they want to be effective. It informs leaders to be directive, supportive, and participative to be achievement oriented. The leadership in the bible was more of directive in the Old Testament especially Moses' style of leadership in most instances and more of participative in the New Testament especially with Jesus' leadership style. The Apostle Paul was more of directive especially where and when he encountered apostasy, heresy or leadership conflicts. However, biblically, the leadership is participatory in nature. Functionally, leadership should be participative for the subordinates to feel their direct contribution to the organization. But when things turn to negative behaviors, attitudes and observance of the signs of compliance, laziness, arrogance and lack of accountability, directive leadership style should be employed to effectively control and turn the tide for the good of the organization. A leader needs to adopt a style that builds subordinate confidence. Path-goal theory questionnaire provides information for respondents about four different leadership style: directive, supportive participative and achievement oriented.

Leadership Styles

Directive leadership- It characterizes a leader who gives subordinates instructions about their tasks, what is expected of them, how to be done and the time limit. A directive leader sets standards of performance and makes the rules and regulations to the employees.

Supportive leader- It is a friendly and approachable leader who attends to the well-being and human needs of subordinates. This kind of a leadership makes sure that there is a good working condition for the employees and treats subordinates as equal. They give high respect for their status.

Participative/Democratic Leadership- This leadership invites subordinates to share and participate in decision making. The leadership consults with subordinates, tapes their views, ideas and opinions and then integrates with theirs to make meaningful decisions for the organization.

Achievement-Oriented Leadership- It is characterized by a leader who challenges the subordinates to perform to the best of their abilities. The leader sets goals of excellence and seeks continuous improvement. He/she shows a high degree of confidence for the subordinates and the potential face all kinds of challenges in order to meet their goals.

House and Mitchell suggest that leaders may exhibit any or all of these four styles. Leaders adapt the style of leadership which can best allow the employees to feel honored and to participate fully to bring the organization to its best performance.

Autocratic/Delegative Leadership – The type of leadership controls, individuals and make decisions of the organization without any input from the employees or from the group members. The type of a leader makes decisions based on individual ideas, perception, judgment and ambitions and shuns advice from anyone or his/her team members. Most of the autocratic leaders are dictators who do not want their team members to contribute and does not listen to any advice but creates rigid rules and structures that allow him/her to be a boss. Such a leader does it all or initiates any creativity in the organization, but dictates policies, procedures, goals and the outcomes which depend on his/her own ability.

Laissez-faire/Delegative Leadership – This type of leadership allows the employees to lead and manage the organization alone without much input from the managers and directors. It is a hands-off approach that allows the subordinates to set the rules and goals and decisions with freedom to do whatever they deem good in their own eyes. It is the leadership that allows things to role on their own, to let it be.

Servant Leadership – This is the type of leadership that demands humility to serve. It is a self-less leadership in which the leader focuses on the welfare of the subordinates and the communities. Servant Leadership, according to Strauch, is one who serves and has child-like heart and humility. Jesus showed humility by washing the feet of His disciples. The proud have no share in the kingdom of God. The servant leader has the moral authority and power to lead and serve the people's needs. Servant leadership entails leadership with humility, empathetic, art of persuasion and thick-listening, soft charact but with strong principles, vision and foresight of the future, and great stewardship abilities and being aware that you are to serve people not to be served.

CHAPTER TWO
POLITICAL LEADERS

P olitical leaders are mostly judged as egocentric, pursuing their private agendas to amass wealth and resources and make their consanguinity to rule the populace. The judgement comes out of the previous political leaders who have taken advantages of their position and access of the natural, human and country's resources available only to those who belong to the cronies of the ruling class. However, they are some exceptional leaders who stand out in human history and show-case the servanthood leadership. They bring their servanthood leadership skills to the spotlight to earn respect, dignity and aptitudes exemplified their leadership by focusing on the people, the community and the nation. Although it is a hypothetical assumption to allude that there is no perfect leader without fault, although that can bring intense scrutiny from other circles. However, the world will agree and affirm some of the following world leaders who were sympathetic and empathetic with the people they led. I invite you to explore with me the political leaders who stood out in human history.

A. Leaders with Positive Influence

Abraham Lincoln - The question is posed, are leaders born of made? Abraham Lincoln is regarded as a political icon who changed the American history. Abraham Lincoln was born on Febraury12, 1809 in Kentucky. Abraham Lincoln was the 16th U.S. President. "a self-taught lawyer, legislator and vocal opponent of slavery, was elected 16th president of the United States in November 1860, shortly before the outbreak of the Civil War. Lincoln proved to be a shrewd military strategist and a savvy leader: His Emancipation Proclamation paved the way for slavery's abolition, while his Gettysburg Address stands as one of the most famous pieces of oratory in American history."[6]

Abraham Lincoln is internationally, revered as an icon leader who brought change in the America history when it comes to his Emancipation Proclamation which ultimately led to the abolition of slavery. "In April 1865, with the Union on the brink of victory, Abraham Lincoln was assassinated by Confederate sympathizer John Wilkes Booth. Lincoln's assassination made him a martyr to the cause of liberty, and he is widely regarded as one of the greatest presidents in U.S. history."[7] Abraham Lincoln died in April 15, 1865 in Washington DC, after being assassinated.

Nelson Mandela – Nels n Mandela was a great stateman, philanthropist and a South African anti-apartheid revolutionary. He was a servant and selfless leader who was brave to confront the apartheid region headlong. Born on July 18, 1918, and served the first black South African President and ushered a new era in South Africa, establishing Truth & Reconciliation Commission led by Anglican Bishop, Desmond Tutu. His spirit of forgiveness and reconciliation to birth a new South African nation, with a rainbow flag, symbolizing the coming together of different peoples within the country to make a one united country, vibrated across the globe to earn him Peace Noble Price.

Nelson Mandela spent twenty-seven years in prison for being a political

---

[6] H History, https://www.history.com/topics/us-presidents/abraham-lincoln, (accessed, July 19, 2021, p. 1).

[7] Ibid. p. 1.

icon to crumble apartheid system that was designed to subjugate, oppress, dehumanize, degrade, exploit, and demean black population in South Africa while promoting and systematizing white supremacy. Almost the whole world condemned the apartheid system. He endured treason trials. "Nelson Mandela never wavered in his devotion to democracy, equality and learning. Despite terrible provocation, he never answered racism with racism. His life is an inspiration to all who are oppressed and deprived; and to all who are opposed to oppression and deprivation. He died at his home in Johannesburg on 5 December 2013."[8] Nelson Mandela will go in the history of humanity as a political icon, humble, articulate, revolutionary and a peace-loving gentleman.

Mahatma Gandhi – Mahatma Gandhi was born in October 2, 1869, in India and he was a lawyer, "an anti-colonialists, nationalist and political ethicist who employed nonviolent resistance to lead the successful campaign for India's independence from British rule and in turn inspired movements for civil rights and freedom across the world."[9] He is known for advocating the doctrine of non-violence protest to attain political and social progress with peaceful means. He resorted to live a life of celibacy although he had fathered four children and began to fast and also became a vegetarian. He began to live a life of poverty. Gandhi abandoned the Western dress for a traditional Indian garb.

Mahatma Gandhi advocated the change of the labor and marriage laws in South Africa for Indians and Indian independence from Britain with a peace and nonviolence means. He inspired so many people in the world and in India to make him both the civil and the political icon. "Gandhi began urging Indians to make their own clothing rather than buy British goods. This would create employment for millions of Indian peasants during the many idle months of the year. He cherished the ideal of economic independence for each village. He identified industrialization (increased use of machines) with materialism (desire for wealth) and felt that it stunted man's growth. Gandhi believed that the individual should

---

[8] https://www.nelsonmandela.org/content/page/biography, (Accessed July 30, 2021).

[9] https://www.google.com/search?q=mahatma+gandhi+biography, (Accessed July, 30, 2021).

be placed ahead of economic productivity."[10] Mahatma Gandhi died on 30 January 1948, after he was assassinated in Delhi by a Hindu fanatic.

Martin Luther King Jr. – Martin Luther King Jr., a civil rights movement activist and religious leader. Born on January 15, 1929, and his original name was Michael Luther King Jr. but his name was changed to Martin Luther King Jr. He was an eloquent speaker against the systematic racism against the blacks and people of color. "In the eleven-year period between 1957 and 1968, King traveled over six million miles and spoke over twenty-five hundred times, appearing wherever there was injustice, protest, and action; and meanwhile he wrote five books as well as numerous articles. In these years, he led a massive protest in Birmingham, Alabama, that caught the attention of the entire world, providing what he called a coalition of conscience."[11]

Martin Luther King Jr., was passionate about black consciousness and inspired so many people across the aisle and became a famous and icon for civil rights movement and he fought against injustice, racism, subjugation, discrimination, and dehumanization of blacks. He advocated for equality of everyone, black and white, and all races. "At the age of thirty-five, Martin Luther King, Jr., was the youngest man to have received the Nobel Peace Prize. When notified of his selection, he announced that he would turn over the prize money of $54,123 to the furtherance of the civil rights movement. On the evening of April 4, 1968, while standing on the balcony of his motel room in Memphis, Tennessee, where he was to lead a protest march in sympathy with striking garbage workers of that city, he was assassinated."[12]

Winston Churchill – Winston Churchill was born in Blenheim Palace, Oxford shire, England on November 30, 1874. He is regarded as a statesman who was pivotal in leading his country, the British, during

---

[10] https://www.fcps.net/site/handlers/filedownload.ashx?moduleinstanceid=19718&dataid=18252&FileName=gandhi.pdf, (Accessed, July 30, 2021).

[11] https://www.nobelprize.org/prizes/peace/1964/king/biographical/, (Accessed, July 31, 2021.

[12] https://www.nobelprize.org/prizes/peace/1964/king/biographical/, (Accessed, July 31, 2021

World War II to victory from the brink of defeat. Winston Churchill was an author, orator, political icon and a statesman who put the British on the world map. He challenged Adolf Hitler and became a prominent leader in the British frontiers during the World War II in the early 1940s. He brought into his circles, Franklin D. Roosevelt, and American President and Joseph Stalin of Russian, the Soviet Union into a coalition, an Alliance to defeat Adolf Hitler in the second World War. He was forced to resign because of his ill health after leading his Conservatives Party to take the reign in 1951. "In Churchill's veins ran the blood of both of the English-speaking peoples whose unity, in peace and war, it was to be a constant purpose of his to promote."[13] Churchill positioned himself to ascend to leadership as opportunity availed itself. He saw a leadership vacuum and filled it with a purpose.

"In a sense, the whole of Churchill's previous career had been a preparation for wartime leadership. An intense patriot; a romantic believer in his country's greatness and its historic role in Europe, the empire, and the world; a devotee of action who thrived on challenge and crisis; a student, historian, and veteran of war; a statesman who was master of the arts of politics, despite or because of long political exile; a man of iron constitution, inexhaustible energy, and total concentration, he seemed to have been nursing all his faculties so that when the moment came he could lavish them on the salvation of Britain and the values he believed Britain stood for in the world."[14]

Winston Churchill was, "a gifted journalist, a biographer and historian of classic proportions, an amateur painter of talent, an orator of rare power, a soldier of courage and distinction, Churchill, by any standards, was a man of rare versatility… In this capacity, at the peak of his powers, he united in a harmonious whole his liberal convictions about social reform, his deep conservative devotion to the legacy of his nation's history, his unshakable resistance to tyranny from the right or from the left, and his capacity to look beyond Britain to the larger Atlantic community and the

---

[13] https://www.britannica.com/biography/Winston-Churchill, (Accessed August 5, 2021).

[14] https://www.britannica.com/biography/Winston-Churchill/Leadership-during-World-War-II, (Accessed August 5, 2021).

ultimate unity of Europe."[15] Winston Church became the British Prime Minster two times, from 1940 to 1945 and again in 1951 to 1955. He was an educated soldier, a Noble price-winner for his writings, a historian, a prolific painter and was one of longest-serving politician in history of Britain. He is regarded as "a man of destiny." He shaped the political landscape of his time during the I World War and II World War. He died on January 24, 1965 at 90 years old in Kensington, London, England. He is remembered as a political icon by his strong will, fighting and defending his country at any cost.

Napoleon Bonaparte- "Napoleon Bonaparte (1769-1821), also known as Napoleon I, was a French military leader and emperor who conquered much of Europe in the early 19th century. Born on the island of Corsica, Napoleon rapidly rose through the ranks of the military during the French Revolution (1789-1799)."[16] They were eight siblings born of a father who was a lawyer, Carlo Buonaparte and mother, Letizia Romalino Buonaparte. The family was not wealthy even though they belonged in a minor Corsican nobility. As a boy, Napoleon learned French language while he was at school and graduated from French military academy in 1785.

"In 1793, following a clash with the nationalist Corsican governor, Pasquale Paoli (1725-1807), the Bonaparte family fled their native island for mainland France, where Napoleon returned to military duty."[17] Napoleon befriended Augustin Robbespierre, the bother of the revolution leader, Maximilien Robespierre. He was a Jacobin, a key figure behind Reign of Terror. Napoleon was under house arrest for his association to the brothers. Napoleon assisted in deflecting the royal insurrection in 1795 against revolution government. With that move, Napoleon was promoted to major general. In 1796, Napoleon commanded the army to defeat the large Austria's armies which was the chief rival of France. "The Directory, the five-person group that had governed France since 1795, offered to let

---

[15] https://www.britannica.com/biography/Winston-Churchill/As-prime-minister-again, (Accessed August 5, 2021).

[16] https://www.history.com/topics/france/napoleon, (Accessed September 28, 2021).

[17] Ibid.

Napoleon lead an invasion of England. Napoleon determined that France's naval forces were not yet ready to go up against the superior British Royal Navy. Instead, he proposed an invasion of Egypt in an effort to wipe out British trade routes with India. Napoleon's troops scored a victory against Egypt's military rulers, the Mamluks, at the Battle of the Pyramids in July 1798."[18] The coup of 18 Brumaire, in which, Napoleon was part of, succeeded in overthrowing the French Directory. The defeat of Austrian strong and being driven out of Italy endorsed Napoleon as the architect of war.

"Napoleon worked to restore stability to post-revolutionary France. He centralized the government; instituted reforms in such areas as banking and education; supported science and the arts; and sought to improve relations between his regime and the pope (who represented France's main religion, Catholicism), which had suffered during the revolution... One of his most significant accomplishments was the Napoleonic Code, which streamlined the French legal system and continues to form the foundation of French civil law to this day."[19] The amendment of the constitution resulted in Napoleon as the consul for life in 1802. After fighting many wars, Napoleon resorted to economic warfare against the British, by creating the Continental System of European port blockades against British trade. Napoleon established for himself, the French aristocracy, and expanded his empire across Western and central continental Europe.

When Russia withdrew from the Continental System in 1810, Napoleon retaliated by invading Russia in the summer of 1812. Instead of confronting the French army, the Russian adopted a strategy of retreating, they burned the cities to cut the supply for the French army to starve to death. The bitter winter of Russian forced the French army to go back to France but brutal loss of lives. "During the disastrous retreat, his army suffered continual harassment from a suddenly aggressive and merciless Russian army. Of Napoleon's 600,000 troops who began the campaign, only an estimated 100,000 made it out of Russia... This loss was followed in 1813 by the Battle of Leipzig, also known as the Battle of Nations, in which Napoleon's forces were defeated by a coalition that included

---

[18] Ibid.

[19] Ibid.

Austrian, Prussian, Russian and Swedish troops. Napoleon then retreated to France, and in March 1814 coalition forces captured Paris."[20] In 1814, Napoleon abdicated the throne and he exiled to Elba, an island in the Mediterranean off the cost of Italy. Napoleon was given a sovereignty of the island. It was less than a year in exile when Napoleon escaped the island to the French mainland with some supporters. He was received warmly by a large crowd which cheering and hailing his name. "The new king, Louis XVIII (1755-1824), fled, and Napoleon began what came to be known as his Hundred Days campaign."[21]

After launching various wars against many European countries, Napoleon was once again forced to abdicate. "In October 1815, Napoleon was exiled to the remote, British-held island of Saint Helena, in the South Atlantic Ocean. He died there on May 5, 1821, at age 51, most likely from stomach cancer. Napoleon was buried on the island despite his request to be laid to rest "on the banks of the Seine, among the French people I have loved so much." In 1840, his remains were returned to France and entombed in a crypt at Les Invalides in Paris, where other French military leaders are interred."[22] Some of Napoleon's quotes:

"The only way to lead people is to show them a future: a leader is a dealer in hope."

"Never interrupt your enemy when he is making a mistake."

"Envy is a declaration of inferiority."

"The reason most people fail instead of succeed is they trade what they want most for what they want at the moment."

"If you wish to be a success in the world, promise everything, deliver nothing."

Joshua Mqabuko Nkomo – Joshua Mqabuko Nkomo was born on June 19, 1917, in Semokwe, in Matabeleland in Zimbabwe. He was a Black nationalist and a leader of Zimbabwe African People's Union (ZAPU). "Nkomo was the son of a teacher and lay preacher in Matabeleland, residing among the Ndebele (formerly called Matabele) and the Kalanga

---

[20] Ibid.

[21] Ibid.

[22] Ibid.

peoples. (Most members of his ZAPU party belonged to the Ndebele, who form the dominant ethnic group in the southern part of the country.) After primary schooling in Rhodesia, he went to South Africa to complete his education in Natal and Johannesburg. Upon returning home in 1945, he worked for the Rhodesian Railways and by 1951 had become a leader in the trade union of the Black Rhodesian railway workers. In 1951 he also obtained an external B.A. degree from the University of South Africa, Johannesburg."[23]

When he completed his studies in South Africa in 1945 and he started work at Rhodesian Railways. As he saw social injustices against the blacks, Joshua Nkomo became more active in politics, rising to be a leader of Trade Unions in 1951. With his leadership skills and charisma, he was elected President of African National Congress (ANC) in 1957 but by 1959, ANC was banned. He escaped imprisonment by going to England. When he returned, he formed National Democratic Party (NDP) in 1960. National Democratic Party (NDP) was also banned in 1961. However, Joshua Nkomo was determined to make sure that he formed a formidable party that would stand against wrath of political regime that was determined to thwart any political parties that waged war against the regime. When NDP was banned in 1961, he then formed Zimbabwe African People Union (ZAPU) in 1961. They incarnated him for ten years from 1964 to 1974 by the white minority government. After he was released from prison, he travelled extensively in Africa and Europe, campaigning for support and advocating and promote African people's rights to vote on one man one vote, equality, equal distribution of land and many other rights that the Africans were denied. Joshua Nkomo led a guerilla warfare and Zimbabwe African National Union (ZANU) led by Robert Mugabe, joined alliance, Patriotic Front, to fight the same cause in 1976.

The war intensified in Zimbabwe and Ian Smith had a deal with Bishop Abel Muzorewa, a leader of the United African National Council (UANC), thinking that Dr. Joshua Nkomo the leader of ZAPU and ZIPRA and Robert G. Mugabe, the leader of ZANU and ZANLA would lay down their weapons and join them. But Dr. Joshua Q. Nkomo and Robert G. Mugabe rejected that offer, vehemently. At the election on May

---

[23] https://www.britannica.com/biography/Joshua-Nkomo, (Accessed October, 5, 2021).

28, 1979, Bishop Abel Muzorewa was appointed to be the Prime Minister of Zimbabwe Rhodesia and Josiah Zion Gumede, my aunt's husband was elected as the first President of Zimbabwe-Rhodesia, (https://en.wikipedia. org/wiki/Lancaster House Agreement, Accessed on December 10, 2020). Rev. Ndabaningi Sithole and Chief Chirau became part of Bishop Abel Muzorewa government. The Rhodesian Front members served under the Prime Minister, Bishop Abel Muzorewa. The government of Bishop Abel Muzorewa, a United Methodist Church Bishop and a nationalist leader, was short-lived in 1979. Dr. Joshua Nkomo and Robert Mugabe refused to recognize that deal, (Wikipedia, https://en.wikipedia.org/wiki/Abel Muzorewa, Accessed on December 13, 2020).

There was a negotiation of the deal which was intended to transfer power, peacefully, from Ian Smith's government, a white minority to black majority. However, it was perceived to be a sinister deal and the Patriotic Party did not become part of the deal. Instead, they continued to wage the war of liberation of independence despite an offer. The internal settlement was also condemned by the United Nations Security Council Resolution 423. There was a Lancaster House Agreement to renegotiate a peaceful deal of independence. Dr. Joshua Nkomo and Robert Mugabe attended the conference under the "Patriotic Front" (PF). It was at Lancaster House Agreement in 1979 negotiation that led to full democracy which ushered parliamentary and Presidential elections and Robert G. Mugabe emerged as a winner on March 24, 1980. He became the Prime Minister of Zimbabwe in 1980 to 1987 and the President until 2017. The elections in 1980 set tribal wars and divisions between the Shona and the Ndebele people to this very day, (https://www.britannica.com/topic/Robert-Mugabe-on-Zimbabwe-1985189/The-Lancaster-House-Negotiations, Accessed on December 15, 2020).

The leader of PF-ZAPU, Dr. Joshua Q. Nkomo was also hunted and he was nearly killed when the 5th Brigade soldiers invaded his house at Number Six in Bulawayo, near the White City. They shot his house and Dr. Joshua Nkomo narrowly escaped murder and he travelled and crossed to Botswana and ended in Britain to seek refuge. He survived the murder plots. The Catholics and Anglican Churches and other churches and human rights started raising voices against that madness of killings. Through talks and negotiations, Dr. Joshua M. Nkomo was persuaded to come back home from Britain. They tried to reconcile with President Mugabe and to negotiate a peace deal but the damage had been done, thousands and thousands of the Ndebeles were dead, women raped and had children of the 5th Brigade forces, and not accounted for. Some people were maimed, some disabled, some traumatized, some imprisoned and some left to suffer emotionally and psychologically for the rest of their lives. The killings stopped on December 22, 1987, when the two, President Robert Mugabe from ZANU-PF and Dr. Joshua Nkomo from PF-ZAPU signed the peace agreement. Dr. Joshua Nkomo was made the second Vice President of Zimbabwe and he entered the agreement to stop the annihilation of the Ndebele Tribe. Peaceful environment prevailed and the reconciliation paid off. It was the wisdom of Dr. Joshua Nkomo to stop the atrocities of Robert Mugabe's government. No harassment and killings publicly from then except secretly adaptions and killings that have continued to this day. Those who had fled the country were given amnesty to come back home and to surrender all their weapons and they were assured of security and protection by all means.

"In 1990 Nkomo became a vice president under Mugabe, but Nkomo was only a figurehead in this position; genuine political power was wielded by Mugabe, who remained Zimbabwe's chief executive. In 1996 Nkomo was diagnosed with prostate cancer. His deteriorating health forced him to retreat from public life, although he continued to hold the title of vice president until his death in 1999."[24]

B. Leaders with Negative Influence

Adolf Hitler – Adolf Hitler was born on April 20, 1889, in Braunau Am Inn, Austria and his father, Alois born in 1837 as an illegitimate. At the beginning, Adolf used his mother's last name, Schiklgruber. However, by1876, he had his legal last name Hitler from his father. "Although Hitler feared and disliked his father, he was a devoted son to his mother, who died after much suffering in 1907. With a mixed record as a student,

---

[24] https://www.britannica.com/biography/Joshua-Nkomo, (Accessed October 11, 2021).

Hitler never advanced beyond a secondary education."[25] Adolf wanted to be an artist and he had an isolated livelihood as he struggled to claim the meaning of life as he survived by painting postcards, advertisements and scathing whatever that could make move on.

Adolf Hitler continued to pursue military adventures, after some eight weeks of training, Hitler was deployed in October 1914 to Belgium where he participated in the First Battle of Ypres. "He served throughout the war, was wounded in October 1916, and was gassed two years later near Yypres. He was hospitalized when the conflict ended. During the war, he was continuously in the front line as a headquarters runner; his bravery in action was rewarded with the Iron Cross, Second Class, in December 1914, and the Iron Cross, First Class (a rare decoration for a corporal), in August 1918. He greeted the war with enthusiasm, as a great relief from the frustration and aimlessness of civilian life. He found discipline and comradeship satisfying and was confirmed in his belief in the heroic virtues of war."[26]

When he rose to leadership and secured Presidency, Adolf Hitler established himself as a dictator and ruled with an iron fist. It is generally, contended that Adolf Hitler was responsible for starting the World War II at the turn of 21st century. "After January 1945 Hitler never left the Chancellery in Berlin or its bunker, abandoning a plan to lead a final resistance in the south as the Soviet forces closed in on Berlin. In a state of extreme nervous exhaustion, he at last accepted the inevitability of defeat and thereupon prepared to take his own life, leaving to its fate the country over which he had taken absolute command… On April 30 he said farewell to Goebbels and the few others remaining, then retired to his suite and shot himself. His wife took poison. In accordance with his instructions, their bodies were burned."[27] Adolf Hitler will remain in the history of humanity as one the leaders who affected the history of humankind with negative impact with his ideologies and the genocides he instigated, especially to the Jews with his Nazism.

---

[25] https://www.britannica.com/biography/Adolf-Hitler, (Accessed August11, 2021).

[26] https://www.britannica.com/biography/Adolf-Hitler. (Accessed August 11, 2021.

[27] https://www.britannica.com/biography/Adolf-Hitler/Hitlers-place-in-history, (Accessed August 14, 2021.)

He wanted to exterminate the entire race in the Jewish holocaust. In his final will and testament, written just before his suicide in April 1945, he charged the Germans to continue the struggle against the Jews: "Above all, I enjoin the government and the people to uphold the race laws to the limit and to **resist** mercilessly the poisoner of all nations, international Jewry."[28] Hitler's legacy bring tears to many people, especially, the Jews who lost more than 6 million loved ones, according to the various sources. "Open and hidden admirers of Hitler continue to exist (and not only in Germany): some of them because of a malign attraction to the efficacy of evil; others because of their admiration of Hitler's achievements, no matter how transitory or brutal. However, because of the brutalities and the very crimes associated with his name, it is not likely that Hitler's reputation as the incarnation of evil will ever change."[29]

Idi Amin – Idi Amin Dada Oumee was born in 24/25 in Kokobo in Uganda who was the President from 1971-1979. His rule was characterized by immense brutality and cruelty. Idi Amin was from a small Kakwa tribe from northwestern Uganda. His background indicates that he had little education. Idi Amin joined the King African Rifles of the British colonial army in 1946 who is said to have been an assistant cook. It is contended that his mother was herbalist or witchdoctor and his father deserted the family, leaving the mother, struggling alone to raise the children.

As a charismatic and influential person, he rose from the military ranks until he overthrew the leader and declared himself the President of Uganda in 1971. "Before Uganda's independence in 1962, Amin became closely associated with the new nation's prime minister and president, Milton Obote. The two men worked to smuggle gold, coffee and ivory out of Congo, but conflicts soon arose between them, and on January 25, 1971, while Obote was attending a meeting in Singapore, Amin staged a successful military coup. Amin became president and chief of the armed forces in 1971, field marshal in 1975 and life president in 1976."[30] Idi Amin became an autocratic leader who lived a lavished lifestyle as President

---

[28] Ibid.

[29] Ibid.

[30] https://www.biography.com/political-figure/idi-amin, (Accessed September 18, 2021).

brought the country into economic collapse at his watch. He clung into power at all cost and committed crime against humanity as many innocent people were massacred.

Idi Amin began his rule by freeing many political prisoners, sent "killer squads" to murder Obote's supporters. His victims included lawyers, journalists, homosexuals, students, and many more who deemed they were his enemies. He gave the Asians 24 hours to vacate Uganda and expelled all of them in 1972 and the country's economy collapsed and never recovered for some decades. He was nicknamed "Butcher of Uganda" because of orchestrating atrocities and brutality to the people of Uganda. His mistake was when he ordered an attack to Tanzania in 1978 and the Tanzanian army which triumphed against the Uganda army. When he realized that the Tanzanian army was closing in against him, he f led to Liberia and then to Saudi Arabia for self-exile in 1979. "On August 16, 2003, Amin died in Jeddah, Saudi Arabia. The cause of death was reported to be multiple organ failure. Although the Ugandan government announced that his body could be buried in Uganda, he was quickly buried in Saudi Arabia. He was never tried for gross abuse of human rights."[31] His legacy is brutality, torture, atrocities, crime against humanity and cruelty to his own people.

Mao Ze Dong – "Mao Tse-tung (also spelled Zedong) was the principal Chinese Marxist theorist, soldier and statesman who led his nation's Cultural Revolution. Mao Tse-tung served as chairman of the People's Republic of China from 1949 to 1959, and led the Chinese Communist Party from 1935 until his death."[32] Mao Tse-tung was born on December 26, 1893, in the farming community of Shaoshan, in the province of Hunan, China, to a peasant family that had tilled their three acres of land for several generations. His authoritarian father, Mao Zedong, was a prosperous grain dealer, and his mother, Wen Qimei, was a nurturing parent."[33] He grew up in a small village and he little education, as it were. At the age of 13, he began working in the fields to earn a living

---

[31] Ibid.

[32] https://www.biography.com/political-figure/mao-tse-tung, (Accessed September 19, 2021).

[33] Ibid.

22

but he was an ambitious boy. "In 1911, the Xinhua Revolution began against the monarchy, and Mao joined the Revolutionary Army and the Kuomintang, the Nationalist Party. Led by Chinese statesman Sun Yat-sen, the Kuomintang overthrew the monarchy in 1912 and founded the Republic of China."[34] Mao Zedong became a certified teacher in 1918 and he travelled to Beijing seeking for a job but he did not succeed. He got a job as a Librarian assistant at the Beijing University while there he heard about Russian Revolution which became communist Soviet Union.

Mao Zedong rose through the ranks. When Chinese President Sun Yat Sen died March 1925, Chiang Kai-Shek succeeded President Sun Yat Sen, and became the chairman of the Kuomintang. Unlike his predecessor, Chiang Kai-Shek was a conservative and traditional and did not want busy as usual. He broke the alliance and started to purge the communists and started to kill them and imprisoning many in 1927. Mao was responsible of helping to establish the Soviet Republic of China in mountains of Jiangxi and formed a formidable guerilla army which became so strong and brutal towards any dissents who were antagonistic to party laws. In strategy, when he learned that Chiang Kai-Shek had surrounded the communist guerillas in the mountains and had planned to exterminate them on the surface of China, the Mao Tse-Tung retreated and avoided confrontation.

"For the next 12 months, more than 100,000 Communists and their dependents trekked west and north in what became known as the "Long March" across the Chinese mountains and swampland to Yanan, in northern China. It was estimated that only 30,000 of the original 100,000 survived the 8,000-mile journey. As word spread that the Communists had escaped extermination by the Kuomintang, many young people migrated to Yanan. Here Mao employed his oratory talents and inspired volunteers to faithfully join his cause as he emerged the top Communist leader."[35] Japanese-Chinese conflict in 1937, necessitated Moa's to rise to power as a communist leader. The Japanese invaded China and Chiang Kai-Sheck fled the capital, Nanking. Unable to defeat the Japanese, Ching Kai-Sheck negotiated a truce and support with the communists who fought the Japanese back with Allied forces.

---

[34] Ibid.

[35] https://www.biography.com/political-figure/mao-tse-tung, (Accessed September 25, 2021).

The Japanese were defeated in 1945 and Mao Tse-Tung controlled the whole of China but the country plunged into bloody civil war after America tried to establish coalition government. At Tiananman Square, in Beijing, Mao Tse-Tung declared the establishment of the Republic of China on October 1, 1949. Chiang Kai-Sheck fled to Taiwan to form Republic of China government. Mao Tse-Tung instituted swiping change and established through persuasion, coercion, murder, terror, violence and by all means necessary to exterminate and seize warlord lands, converting it into people's communes. His policies were challenged, criticized, and by "intense rejection by the urban intelligentsia." When Mao realized that his control was slipping away because of his policies, he instigated ruthless laws to crush dissents. Mao Tse-Tun's launch of "Great Leap Forward" in January 1958, in an effort to increase agricultural and industrial production, proved to be a dismal failure due to poor harvest, flood and industrial slump. A historical manmade famine saw over 40 million Chinese die of starvation between 1958-1961. Mao's failure of his "Great Leap Forward" in 1962, he was overtaken and forced to step aside by his rivals.

Mao Tse Tung made his political come back in 1966, in May at the age of 73. He manufactured a problem stating that bourgeois elements wanted to bring capitalism back and that they were the enemy of the state. He campaigned against the bourgeois capitalists that they were responsible and were to be removed. He embraced the youth and gained the popularity again and he was flung into Presidency the second time. His youthful followers organized a purge called "Undesirables" and formed Red Guard under the youth wing. He ordered the closer of all China schools and the young intellectuals were forced leave cities to go and live in the countryside to be "re-educated" through hard labor. "Mao Tse-tung died from complications of Parkinson's disease on September 9, 1976, at the age of 82, in Beijing, China. He left a controversial legacy in both China and the West as a genocidal monster and political genius. Officially, in China, he is held in high regard as a great political strategist and military mastermind, the savior of the nation. However, Mao's efforts to close China to trade and market commerce and eradicate traditional

Chinese culture have largely been rejected by his successors."[36] Are leaders born or made, Mao Tse-Tung gives us a glimpse of one of the leadership models in the world.

Jozef Stalin- Joseph Stalin was born into poverty in December 18, 1878, from a small-town of Gori, Georgia in Russia. Joseph Stalin was born the only child and poor as his father was a shoemaker and an alcoholic and his mother was a laundress. Stalin had smallpox that affected his face and left him with some scars. In his early years, he got a scholarship to attend a seminary to study as a priest in Georgian Orthodox Church. While studying, he got interested in studying German social philosophy and Karl Max's "Communist Manifesto" and became interested in Russian revolution against Russian monarchy. To his demise, Joseph Stalin was expelled from seminary for missing an exam in 1899.

Stalin became a political infiltrator and became involved in strikes and demonstrations and later joined Marxist Social Democratic Movement and gained the nickname, Koba. He was arrested several times and imprisoned in Siberia as he got involved in criminal activities and bank robbery and the proceeded fund and supported Bolshevik Party. "In 1912, Lenin, then in exile in Switzerland, appointed Joseph Stalin to serve on the first Central Committee of the Bolshevik Party. Three years later, in November 1917, the Bolsheviks seized power in Russia."[37] Stalin rose from rank to rank until he was chosen as the secretary general of Central Committee in 1922 of the Communist party a position that enabled him to appoint his friends to high positions who actually became the database for him to lay a strong foundation for his leadership position. "After Lenin died in 1924, Stalin eventually outmaneuvered his rivals and won the power struggle for control of the Communist Party. By the late 1920s, he had become dictator of the Soviet Union… Starting in the late 1920s, Joseph Stalin launched a series of five-year plans intended to transform the Soviet Union from a peasant society into an industrial superpower. His development plan was centered on government control of the economy and included

---

[36] Ibid.

[37] https://www.history.com/topics/russia/joseph-stalin#section, (Accessed September 25, 2021).

the forced collectivization of Soviet agriculture, in which the government took control of farms."[38] The farmers did not comply with Stalin's order but rejected. Stalin killed millions of the farmers who had rejected his order and some were forced to exile.

"Stalin ruled by terror and with a totalitarian grip in order to eliminate anyone who might oppose him. He expanded the powers of the secret police, encouraged citizens to spy on one another and had millions of people killed or sent to the Gulag system of forced labor camps."[39] Stalin built a cult around himself as he ordered cities were renamed in his honor, Soviet Union books were rewritten to capture his concepts and ideology to be incorporated in the school curriculums, history books, literature, artwork and music. All was about him and he controlled social media and the national anthem was about him and his fame. "In 1939, on the eve of World War II, Joseph Stalin and German dictator Adolf Hitler (1889-1945) signed the German-Soviet Nonaggression Pact. Stalin then proceeded to annex parts of Poland and Romania, as well as the Baltic states of Estonia, Latvia and Lithuania. He also launched an invasion of Finland. Then, in June 1941, Germany broke the Nazi-Soviet pact and invaded the USSR, making significant early inroads.[40] Stalin did not take the advice of United States and Britain, seriously about the possible invasion by the Germans. Soon he learned from his mistakes and Adolf Hitler invaded Soviet Union without delay.

Stalin organized his army to confront the enemy headlong without fainting and were able to drive the Germans their infrastructure and their supplies. The Soviet Red Army triumphant at the 'Battle of Stalingrad" in August 1942 to February 1943. "Joseph Stalin did not mellow with age: He prosecuted a reign of terror, purges, executions, exiles to labor camps and persecution in the postwar USSR, suppressing all dissent and anything that smacked of foreign–especially Western–influence. He established communist governments throughout Eastern Europe, and in 1949 led the Soviets into the nuclear age by exploding an atomic bomb. In 1950, he gave North Korea's communist leader Kim Il Sung (1912-1994) permission to

---

[38] Ibid.

[39] Ibid.

[40] Ibid.

invade United States-supported South Korea, an event that triggered the Korean War."[41]

Joseph Stalin used all his power and authority to leave a legacy in Soviet Unions as the architecture of political guru of his time. "Stalin, who grew increasingly paranoid in his later years, died on March 5, 1953, at age 74, after suffering a stroke. His body was embalmed and preserved in Lenin's mausoleum in Moscow's Red Square until 1961, when it was removed and buried near the Kremlin walls as part of the de-Stalinization process initiated by Stalin's successor Nikita Khrushckev (1894-1971). By some estimates, he was responsible for the deaths of 20 million people during his brutal rule."[42]

Benito Mussolini- Benito Mussolini was born on July 29, 1883 in Verano di Costa, Italy by his father, Mussolini, who was a blacksmith and his mother, Rosa Maltoni who was a devout Catholic. Benito Mussolini stabbed a student at the age of 10 years and he was expelled from school. He stabled another student when he was 14 years old and he was suspended from school. Benito Mussolini's family lived a simple life. When he became older, Benito travelled to Switzerland and got involved in protests and demonstration as he had joined the Socialist Party in Switzerland. Benito moved to Austria-Hungary in 1909 and became an editor of a socialist newspaper but his demise came when he was deported because of the violation of the country's laws.

"In 1910, Mussolini became the editor for another socialist newspaper, but soon spent six months in jail for inciting violence. During his incarceration, he began to write his autobiography—while still in his twenties—detailing his troubled school years and his many romantic conquests."[43] In 1914, Mussolini started his own newspaper and encouraged and instigated violence. Mussolini the Italian army in 1915 and he fought in World War 1, but he got wounded. By 1918, Mussolini had returned to newspaper business. "In 1919—and his dissatisfaction with it—Mussolini

---

gathered the various fascist groups into a national organization called Fasci Italian di Combattimento. The Italiniani Fascists courted war veterans and encouraged violence against socialists. Mussolini stockpiled weapons and explosives in his newspaper offices."[44] Mussolini stood in the general election but he lost in the election as a Fascist candidate.

"Two days later, Mussolini was arrested for allegedly collecting arms to overthrow the government. He was released without charges the next day. In 1921, the Italian King Victor Emmanuel III dissolved Parliament amidst growing violence and chaos. Elections brought a huge win for the Fascists, with Mussolini taking a seat as a deputy in Parliament. The party changed its name to Partito Nazionale Fascista."[45] Thereafter, many cities were seized by the Fascists squads and burned down some of the Communists and Socialists buildings. Mussolini threatened to march to Rome to seize the government buildings through violence in 1922.

"Refusing to pass martial law, King Victor Emmanuel III watched as thousands of armed Fascists entered Rome. He dissolved the government and asked Mussolini to form a new one. Mussolini became Prime Minister, as well as Minister of the Interior and Minister for Foreign Affairs."[46] In 1926, the Catholic boys were dissolved, Communists and Socialists were arrested, spelled and some imprisoned. Muss lini befriended Adolf whom he criticized his leaders ip at but they partnered together in anti-Semitics campaign. Meanwhile, Italy invaded Ethiopia in 1935 and Germany seconded the move. "Both Hitler and Mussolini sided with Francisco Franco in the Spanish Civil War in 1936, with Mussolini providing 50,000 troops. In 1937, Italy left the League of Nations in solidarity with Germany and in March of 1938, Hitler invaded Austria with Mussolini's support."[47] Mussolini was closed in by the troops, captured as he was trying escape with his girlfriend.

Mussolini's autopsy indicate that he was killed by firing squad on April 28, 1945. "The bodies of both Mussolini and Petacci were hung upside down at the Piazzale Loreto in Milan and displayed for crowds to kick

---

[44] Ibid.

[45] Ibid.

[46] Ibid.

[47] Ibid.

and spit on. One day later, Hitler Committed suicide and the following week, Germany surrendered."[48] Democracy was restored in Italy after 20 years of dictatorship. Some sources say his brains were collected to research and study the brains of a dictator. Mussolini was a dictator, frown by the history of the world.

Tshaka Zulu – Tshaka was born in 1787, the Zulu chief who later became the king of the Zulu kingdom, the architecture and the founder of Africa's Zulu empire. He is credited with creating a formidable army of warriors who devastated the whole region in Southern Africa. "Shaka was the son of Senzangakona, chieftain of the Zulu, and Nandi, an orphaned princess of the neighboring Langeni clan. Because his parents belonged to the same clan, their marriage violated Zulu custom, and the stigma of this extended to the child. The couple separated when Shaka was six, and Nandi took her son back to the Langeni, where he passed a fatherless boyhood among a people who despised his mother. In 1802 the Langeni drove Nandi out, and she finally found shelter with the Dletsheni, a subclan of the powerful Mthethwa. When Shaka was 23, Dingiswayo, the Mthethwa paramount chieftain, called up Shaka's Dletsheni age group for military service. For the next six years, he served with brilliance as a warrior of the Mthethwa Empire."[49]

When Senzangakona died in 1816, Dingiswayo gave Tshaka the liberty to go and take over the Zulu. When Tshaka took over, it one was one the smallest Eastern Nguni Bantu clans but Tshaka consolidated it and made it a massive, Nguni clans. He ruled with intimidation, murders, killings, and slaughters of those who resisted his rule. He organized the army, giving up oxide's shields, and replacing it with long-bladed, short-halved stabbing assegais, forcing them to fight their enemies in close range, "which forced them to fight at close quarters. He then instituted the regimental system based on age groups, quartered at separate kraals (villages) and distinguished by uniform markings on shields and by various combinations of headdress and ornaments. He developed standard tactics, which the Zulu used in every battle. The available regiments (known

---

[48] Ibid.

[49] https://www.britannica.com/biography/Shaka-Zulu-chief, (Accessed October 11, 2021).

collectively as the impi) were divided into four groups. The strongest, termed the "chest," closed with the enemy to pin him down while two "horns" raced out to encircle and attack the foe from behind. A reserve, known as the "loins," was seated nearby, with its back to the battle so as not to become unduly excited, and could be sent to reinforce any part of the ring if the enemy threatened to break out. The battle was supervised by indunas, or officers, who used hand signals to direct the regiment."[50] Tshaka was merciless, and ruthless, exterminating anyone who resisted his advance.

He first of all decimated the small clans in his vicinity and amalgamated them into his kingdoms and Langeni was his first targets. "He sought out the men who had made his boyhood a misery and impaled them on the sharpened stakes of their own kraal fences. In less than a year, the Zulu—and their army—had quadrupled in number. In 1817 Dingiswayo—still Shaka's overlord—was murdered, and the last restraint on Zulu expansion was removed."[51] The two largest clans, the Ndwandwe and Qhabe, were the last one that he dismantled and left them burning and the survivors in disarray and begging to be Tshaka's subjects in 1823. Mfecane, ("Crushing"), in 1820s, many clans escaped the brutal and atrocious invasions of Tshaka's army which was ruthless, crushing clans who refused to join his kingdom. Many chief clans of various tribes escaped northwards, southwards and eastwards, to find new lands for the people as they could not tolerate the iron hand by now King Tshaka.

The bigger enemies of Tshaka arrived in Zululand, as he on slaughter to expand his kingdom. The Boer Great Trek, passed through Tshaka's kingdom with they advanced weaponry in 1830. "The first Europeans arrived in Port Natal (present-day Durban) in 1824. A dozen settlers of the Farewell Trading Company established a post on the landlocked bay and soon made contact with Shaka, whose kraal Bulawayo lay 100 miles (160 km) to the north. Fascinated by their ways and their artifacts but convinced that his own civilization was much superior, he permitted them to stay. Two of the early settlers, Henry Francis Fynn and Nathaniel Isaacs, became fluent Zulu linguists, and most of what is known of early

---

[50] Ibid.

[51] Ibid.

Nguni history stems from their writings."[52] The death of Tshaka's mother, (INdhlovukazi), began sorrowful events. He loved his mother, dearly and he sought to avenge his childhood struggles toward those who perpetrated his misery.

"In 1827 Nandi died, and with his mother's death Shaka became openly psychotic. About 7,000 Zulus were killed in the initial paroxysm of his grief, and for a year no crops were planted, nor could milk—the basis of the Zulu diet staple—be used. All women found pregnant were slain with their husbands, as were thousands of milch cows, so that even the calves might know what it was to lose a mother. Early in 1828 Shaka sent the impi south in a raid that carried the warriors clear to the borders of the Cape Colony. They had no sooner returned, expecting the usual season's rest, than he sent them off to raid far in the north. It was too much for his associates, and two of his half-brothers, Dingane and Mhlangana, together with an induna named Mbopa, murdered him in September of that year."[53] Tshaka's impact of his kingdom went far and beyond and Southern African regions felt his punch and were in constant fear of his attack. He is known all of the world of his powerful weaponry, that he created and mastered and taught his warries to be fearless and fight with bravery using a short-spear, with the attack of the enemy in a close range. He is widely known and remembered for his brutality, atrocities, massacre and extermination of any opponent to his kingdom, the Zulu kingdom.

---

[52] Ibid.

[53] Ibid.

CHAPTER THREE
LEADERS WITH BIBLICAL INFLUENCE

Barnabas

Barnabas was an interesting character with a powerful testimony about his character, attitude, generosity, teaching and preaching abilities, mentorship, encourager, trusted and an apologist. He is introduced in the book of Acts as Joseph from Cyprus, a very kind and generous man who sold his field and brought the proceeds from the sales on the feet of the Apostles in Jerusalem, (Acts 4:32935, NKJV). He was later nicknamed 'Barnabas' which means, "Son of prophet" in Aramaic. The author of the Book of Acts, Luke, quotes Barnabas as "son of encouragement." He was known as a generous man, full of the Spirit of encouragement and expounding the Word, intelligibly.

Barnabas' Background

He was early converted to Christianity, earlier than Paul. He was a very rich and a generous man. He was known as son of exhortation, encouragement and consolation. Some scholars think that his name, 'Barnabas', originally *Bar-N' bo*, son of Nebo, a Babylonian god. Brand, Draper and England assert, "Barnabas's name appears 23 times in Acts and five times in Paul's letters and probably means "son of prophecy" or one who prophesies or preaches (son of exhortation," Acts 4:36, NKJV). Barnabas in Acts was a Levite native of the island of Cyprus, named Joseph (Jose), before the disciples called him Barnabas."[54] In (Acts 4:36, NJKV), Luke also interprets Barnabas as "son of *parakleesis*', "one who encourages, or exhorts", or "son of peace." "Strictly, this would be 'son of prophet' or 'of prophecy', but exhortation was extremely a prophetic function (Acts 15: 32; I Cor. 14:3, NKJV), and Luke is concerned, not to provide a scientific etymology, but to indicate the man's character."[55] He was a spiritual man and loved by many people. He was a man of peace and love and encouragement.

"He came from a Jewish-Cypriot priestly family, but the Jerusalemite John Mark was his cousin (Col.4:10, NKJV), he himself was the early member of the Jerusalem church, selling his property, (in Cyprus?), for the common good (Acts 4:36ff, NKJV)."[56] Clement of Alexandria has accorded him as one of the seventy. Many scholars regard him as one of the Apostles as alluded by Luke (14:4, 14, NIV). The Apostle Paul also called him an apostle (I Cor. 9:6, NIV). There is an Epistle called the Epistle of Barnabas, according the two cycles of tradition that asserted that Barnabas was the author of the Epistle. However, it has been rejected not having written by Barnabas because of dates. One linked Barnabas with Milan and the other with Cyprus. "It is the late which appears in the *Acts of Barnabas,* probably composed in Cyprus not earlier than 5th Century. The book claims to be written by John Mark (converted by Paul, Barnabas, and Silas and baptized in I conium), and is clearly based on the canonical Acts."[57] It has not been agreed to claim the authorship of Barnabas. The fundamental argument about attaching Barnabas as the author is that "In spite of the opinion of CLEMENT OF ALEXANDRIA and the church fathers, it is highly unlikely that the document has any connection with

---

[54] Chad Brand, Charles Draper and Archie England, Holman Illustrated Bible Dictionary, (Nashville: Holman Press, 2003, 173.

[55] J.D. Douglas, New Bible Dictionary, (England: Inter-Varsity Press, 1996), 123.

[56] Ibid., 123.

[57] Merrill C. Tenney, The Zondervan Encyclopedia of the Bible, (Grand Rapids: Zondervan Publishers, 2009), 510.

Barnabas who is recorded in the book of Acts as a fellow missionary of the apostle Paul. The probable date of its origin is too late for that."[58] Tertullian referred to him as the author of Hebrews. Clementine stated Barnabas as the Mathias of Acts 1:23, 26, NIV. There is no way the Epistle could be assigned to Barnabas because it was well past his time. No more details about Barnabas' earlier life.

Barnabas' Character

Barnabas is characterized as a man of God, spirit-filled, devote, warm-hearted, generous, peaceful, encourager and a mentor. Luke called him a 'good man, full of the Holy Spirit' (Acts 11:24, NIV). Douglas identifies three reasons he was respected as a good man:

a. when the converted Saul arrived in Jerusalem only to discover that the Christians thought he was a spy, it was Barnabas who introduced him to the 'pillar' apostle and convinced them of his conversion and sincerity (Acts 9;27; Gal.1;18, NIV).

b. It was Barnabas who represented the apostles at Antioch when, for the first time Gentiles had been evangelized in significant numbers.

c. Barnabas' third great contribution, however, showed him committed to full acceptance of Gentiles on faith in Christ (Acts 13:46, NKJV).[59]

He was a friend and companion of Paul. He first demonstrated his generosity in the early church when he sold his field and gave the money to the church. He was moderately wealthy. He was able to community with both the Jews and the Gentiles and understood both cultures. He was a kind man and very support of the church and those who led and taught in the church. He is remembered for his outstanding gift of encouragement and diligence in handling complex situations. Barnabas interceded for Paul when the church in Jerusalem was suspicious of him as a Christian persecutor. He became a friend of Paul who was a persecutor of Christians

---

[58] Ibid., 510.

[59] Douglas, 1996, 123.

(Acts 9:270, NIV). They became close associates and friends in advancing the gospel to the Gentiles. Barnabas had leadership qualities and was a mentor. When Paul had refused to take John Mark with them who had deserted them while they were going to Perga, (Acts 13:13, NIV), it was Barnabas who took John Mark with, parting with Paul who took Silas. John Mark was Barnabas' cousin. The two close friends parted ways. "Church tradition identifies Barnabas as a writer .... Nonetheless, Barnabas has always been honored as a great missionary of the church, and many consider him as a latter Apostle."[60]

Barnabas was a man of encouragement and hospitality. He is known for his zealous for the mission work. "In the letter to the Galatians, Paul describes how he and Barnabas were given the 'right hand of fellowship' by the Jerusalem leadership and had their mission to the Gentiles approved. Acts portrays Barnabas as Paul's senior partner in evangelizing Cyprus and I conium until their split over the role of John Mark, (Acts 15:36-41, NKJV)."[61] Barnabas possessed spiritual authority. Barnabas is mentioned over twenty-four times in the book of Acts. He was a godly motivated giver. He had good reputation and integrity. Barnabas was full of faith, holiness honesty, obedient and a great evangelist.

Barnabas' Service and mentorship

Barnabas was a spiritual leader who demonstrated his leadership skills in putting people on the right positions and helping them mature into leadership. The first service of Barnabas is when he linked Paul to the established church in Jerusalem. Barnabas persuaded the church to accept Paul who was the persecutor of Christ's church. He helped Paul to ascend to leadership position in the church. As the son of encouragement, Barnabas did not doubt Paul's conversion and he quickly accepted him, demystifying suspension from the apostles in the church. "As a result of Barnabas' endorsement, Paul stayed with them and moved about freely in

---

[60] Richard R. Losch, All the People in the Bible, (Grand Rapids: William B. Eerdmans Publishers, 2008), 58.

[61] Bruce M. Metzger and Michael D. Coogan, The Oxford guide to places of the Bible, (Oxford: University Press, 2001), 31.

Jerusalem, speaking boldly in the name of the Lord" (Acts 9:28, NIV). Barnabas was a divine contact for Paul."[62]

Barnabas also linked Paul with the church in Antioch. He had a very fruitful ministry in Antioch church. He encouraged the church to remain faithful to the Lord with all their hearts" (Acts 11:23, NIV). When the church grew more and more in Antioch, Barnabas observed that he needed someone to help him. So, he asked Paul if he could come to join him (Acts 11:25, NIV). Paul had spent six years in Tarsus. He incorporated Paul into the leadership team of the apostles and teachers in Antioch church under Barnabas leadership, (Acts 13:1, NIV). They spent the whole year teaching and instructing together in the church of Antioch. This was Barnabas' display of leadership authority. He mentored Paul to be credible teacher. Both Barnabas and Paul became great teachers of the Word in Antioch and it was the impact and effectiveness of their roles as great teachers, preachers and evangelists that the disciples were first called "Christians" in Antioch, (Acts 11:26, NIV). Barnabas' leadership qualities were observed again as he championed the Antioch's response to Judea's famine. He encouraged the disciples in Antioch to contribute and help the disciples in Judean church when the church was having needs for food. It was Barnabas and Saul who were sent to deliver the gifts to the disciples living in Judea (Acts11:29, NIV). Barnabas was having a gift of evangelism, teaching and giving and he also inspired all those who were under him.

Barnabas was a man of integrity and responsibility. "Upon his arrival Barnabas 'saw the evidence of the grace of God' at work in the lives of the news believers and it gladdened his heart (Acts 11:23a, NKJV). He fixed his attention not on the eating habits, cultural distinctive, and external appearances, but on the transformed life-orientation brought about by their encounter with Jesus."[63] Barnabas was humble enough to be eclipsed by Paul in terms of teaching. He was called an "apostle," though not one of the twelve. "In (I Cor. 9:6, NKJV), Paul refers to Barnabas as a

---

[62] Stephen B. Bond, Spiritual Authority: God's Way of Growing Leaders, (Joplin: College Publishers, 1995), 127.

[63] Don N. Howell, Jr., Servants of Servant: A Biblical Theology of Leadership, (Eugene, Oregon: Wipf & Stock Publishers, 2003), 232.

self-supporter, like himself."[64] According to (Acts 12:2, NKJV), the Holy Spirit first called Barnabas and then Paul. God knew before-hand that Paul would Barnabas to train and mentor him into becoming the great teacher. Barnabas was referred as a prophet and a teacher in Acts 13:1, NKJV). "As a prophet, Barnabas likely spoke in response to the moving Spirit, providing edification, exhortation, and consolation. The Spiritual gift of prophecy can be added to the list of other gifts we have seen in his life (i.e., encouragement, giving, evangelism, and teaching. Truly, Barnabas was a highly gifted servant of God."[65] He was a man of fasting and prayer. He was obedient to the direction of the Holy Spirit. He demonstrated servant leadership qualities.

When a circumcision conflict arose in Antioch church in Jerusalem, brought by the legalistic Jews from Judea, Barnabas stood with Peter and James against Paul (Acts 15:2, NKJV). Barnabas had a great influence in the resolution in the Jerusalem council. The issue was whether the Gentiles believers should observe the Jewish customs and traditions which included circumcision to become full members of the church or not. Paul's position was to teach and preach the gospel of grace. He overlooked the mistakes made by John Mark, his cousin who deserted them when they were going to Perga. He embraced the weak and encouraged them to move on and work for the Lord. He wanted everyone to prosper in his ways to fulfill God's purpose. But the conflict between himself and Paul over John Mark had a long-lasting impact on both of them. But interesting enough, at the end, Paul had to call John Mark to come to help him when he was in prison, (Col. 4:10, NKJV). "Get Mark and bring him with you, because he is helpful to me in my ministry, (2: Tim. 4:11, NKJV). Barnabas had taught and mentored Mark to the extent that Paul in his last days in prison saw that Mark was helpful in his ministry because of what Barnabas had invested in Mark earlier in his life for the Lord. He was a good man and he embraced the failed brother. "Leadership developing for Christian ministry involves the growth and maturing of the emerging leaders, under the direction of God's Spirit, in order that they might be prepared for effective

---

[64] George Alexander, The Handbook of Biblical Personalities, (Greenwich: Seabury Press, 1962.

[65] Bond, 1995, 128.

servant leadership."[66] There were some differences of character and gifts, between Paul and Barnabas. Paul was a great teacher and missionary and while Barnabas was a great teacher and leader but with passion for people and their weaknesses. "Teacher's shape, challenge, and change people, and in doing so, they lead. Great teachers are leaders, and conversely, great leaders must be teachers."[67]

Barnabas as a Teacher and an Apologist

The distinction between Barnabas and Paul comes when they were at Lystra and they were thought to be gods in the likeness of men. Barnabas was called Zeus and Paul was called Hermes. Howell contends, "Barnabas is equated with Zeus, the fatherly head of the Greek pantheon. Zeus, (the Roman Jupiter) can intervene in human affairs with ferocity in tempest, thunder and lightning, but more often orchestrates activity of gods, behaving like a king than a tyrant. Hermes (the Roman Mercury) is the chief spokesman who carries out instructions of Zeus with speed and diligence."[68] Barnabas being referred to as Zeus was held as a leader and mentor while they referred to Paul as Hermes, a great speaker. They had lived and worked together in Antioch church for five years and all together seven years, including as missionaries together. They worked peacefully, until they had a dispute over Mark. Barnabas and Paul united under the pressure of some Judaizers who had infiltrated the church and demanded the Gentile believers to be circumcised and to observe the Law of Moses. They defended and taught the justification by grace alone not by keeping the Mosaic Law (Acts 15:1, 2, NKJV). He was a seasoned teacher who demonstrated the knowledge of understanding of the Scriptures so deep and with sound interpretations. He was both filled with the Spirit and the knowledge of the cross.

Barnabas was a great leader who imparted his skills and talents to so many people, including Paul and John Mark. Woolfe asserts, "But leaders of the Bible, who rarely used the term, 'team' were masters of

---

[66] Michael J. Anthony and James Estep Jr., *Management Essentials for Christian Ministries,* (Nashville: B & C Publishers, 2005), 297.

[67] Gary Bredfeldt, Great Leader Great Teacher, (Chicago: Moody Publishers, 2006), 13.

[68] Howell, 2003, 233.

team practice."[69] Barnabas formed the strong team of missionaries who preached to the Gentile fields. He saw beyond to form a team instead of working alone. "The stage of performance management consists of helping people set ambitious yet realistic goals and motivating them toward the achievement of those goals."[70] Barnabas was one who had discernment and encouraged those whom he saw having great potential as teachers and preachers like Paul, John Mar and Silas. In contrast to Paul, Barnabas had numerous gifts including that of encouraging and mentoring. "The best modern leaders also place strong value on people. They also realize that references to a 'team' right hollow if members of the team don't feel valued as people, or if they see the team leader reaping all the glory while they do all the work."[71] Kouzes and Posner reiterate this point, "Collaboration is the critical competency for achieving and sustaining high performance, especially in the Internet Age! It won't be the ability to fiercely compete but the ability to loving and cooperate that will determine success."[72] Barnabas was an exemplary leader who followed the footsteps of Jesus Christ.

Barnabas is introduced in the book of Acts as Joseph from Cyprus, a very kind and generous man who sold his field and brought the proceeds from the sales on the feet of the Apostles in Jerusalem, (Acts 4:32935, NIV). The author of the Book of Acts, Luke, quotes Barnabas as "son of encouragement." He was known as a generous man, full of the Spirit of encouragement and expounding the Word, intelligibly. He has a powerful testimony about his character, attitude, generosity, teaching and preaching abilities, mentorship, encourager, trusted and an apologist. Barnabas interceded for Paul when the church in Jerusalem was suspicious of him as a Christian persecutor. He overlooked the mistakes made by John Mark, his cousin who deserted them when they were going to Perga. He embraced the weak and encouraged them to move on and work for the Lord. Barnabas' leadership qualities were observed again as he championed

---

[69] Lorin woolfe, *Leadership Secrets from the Bible*, (New York: MJF Books Publishers, 2002), 130.

[70] Ibid. 111.

[71] Ibid. 131.

[72] James M. Kouzes and Barry Z. Posner, *Leadership Challenge, 3rd*, (San Francisco: Jossey –Bass Publishers, 2003), 141.

the Antioch's response to Judea's famine. He encouraged the disciples in Antioch to contribute and help the disciples in Judean church when the church was having needs for food. Barnabas was a good leader who teaches every leader to be humble, generous, God-fearing, good teacher and preacher, mentor, full of power and authority and filled with the Holy Spirit.

William Carey – William Carey was born on August 17, 1761 in Paulersbury, Northampton shire, England. "William was the Carey was the founder of the English Baptist Missionary Society 1792. "At the age of 14, Carey's father apprenticed him to a cordwainer in the nearby village of Piddington, Northampton shire. His master, Clarke Nichols, was a churchman like himself, but another apprentice, John Warr, was a Dissenter. Through his influence Carey would leave the Church of England and join with other Dissenters to form a small Congregational church in nearby Hackleton. While apprenticed to Nichols, he also taught himself Greek with the help of Thomas Jones, a local weaver who had received a classical education."[73] William and Dorothy Carey had seven children, five sons and two daughters; both girls died when they were young and their son, Peter. He began his life in the humble beginnings.

Carey got involved with Particular Baptists and John Ryland, John Sutcliff and Andrew Fuller who became close friends. They appointed him to be the schoolmaster and he became a Pastor in a local church. William Carey preached one of the greatest sermons, of all times, entitled, "Expect great things from God; attempt great things for God." Baptist Missionary World Missions was founded in October, 1792, by Carey, Andrew Fuller, John Ryland, and John Sutcliff who became the charter members. Dr. John Thomas, a medical missionary was in England to raising funds. William Carey would go to India as missionaries. "Carey, his eldest son Felix, Thomas and his wife and daughter sailed from London aboard an English ship in April 1793. Dorothy Carey had refused to leave England, being pregnant with their fourth son and having never been more than a few miles from home; but before they left, they asked her again to come with them and she gave consent, with the knowledge that her sister Kitty

---

[73] https://en.wikipedia.org/wiki/William_Carey_(missionary), (Accessed October, 18, 2021.

would help her give birth."[74] The missionary society had begun to send more and more missionaries and the mission work began to grow in India. "The first to arrive was John Fountain, who arrived in Midnapore and began teaching. He was followed by William Ward, a printer; Joshua Marshman, a schoolteacher; David Brunsdon, one of Marshman's students; and William Grant, who died three weeks after his arrival. Because the East India Company was still hostile to missionaries, they settled in the Danish colony in Serampore and were joined there by Carey on 10 January 1800."[75] The mission bought a house in Serampore which accommodated all the families. They also bought a school that was meant to support the mission work in India and their families. "In 1808 Carey remarried. His new wife Charlotte Rhumohr, a Danish member of his church was, unlike Dorothy, Carey's intellectual equal. They were married for 13 years until her death."[76] Bengal that was physically, politically and spiritually, was very difficult to preach in as the indigenous resisted the gospel.

William Carey was assessed and evaluated about his writings and articles of Indian people. Some of his writings describing the Indian people was scrutinized. "According to Indian historian V. Rao, Carey lacked understanding and respect for Indian culture, with him describing Indian music as "disgusting" and bringing to mind practices "dishonorable" to God. Such attitudes affected the literature authored by Carey and his colleagues… Biographies of Carey, such as those by F. D. Walker and J. B. Myers, only allude to Carey's distress caused by the mental illness and subsequent breakdown suffered by his wife, Dorothy, in the early years of their ministry in India. More recently, Beck's biography of Dorothy Carey paints a more detailed picture: William Carey uprooted his family from all that was familiar and sought to settle them in one of the most unlikely and difficult cultures in the world for an uneducated eighteenth, century English peasant woman. Faced with enormous difficulties in adjusting to all of this change, she failed to make the adjustment emotionally and ultimately, mentally, and her husband seemed to be unable to help her through all of this because he just did not know what to do about it…

---

[74] Ibid.

[75] https://en.wikipedia.org/wiki/William_Carey_(missionary), (Accessed October 23, 2021).

[76] Ibid.

Dorothy's mental breakdown ("at the same time William Carey was baptizing his first Indian convert and his son Felix, his wife was forcefully confined to her room, raving with madness") led inevitably to other family problems."[77] Carey was not able to balance between his family and the mission work. He was caring more about the mission work rather the health of his wife.

Besides the neglect of his wife who suffered mental health at his hand, William Carey contributed a lot in the mission work in India. "Carey devoted great efforts and time to the study not only of the common language of Bengali, but to many other Indian vernaculars including the ancient root language of Sanskrit. In collaboration with the College of Fort William, Carey undertook the translation of the Hindu classics into English, beginning with the three-volume epic poem the Ramayana. He then translated the Bible into Bengali, Oriya, Marathi, Hindi, Assamese, Sanskrit and parts of it into other dialects and languages. For 30 years Carey served in the college as the professor of Bengali, Sanskrit and Marathi, publishing, in 1805, the first book on Marathi grammar."[78] This is incredible commitment and contribution in the kingdom of God in India.

William Carey was the founder of English Baptist Missionary Society who was a lifelong missionary to India. He set a pattern for model missionary work in Indian and the whole missionary work in the world. He is called the "Father of Bengali prose," because his commitment and dedication of mission work in Bengali in India, including his work in translations to the local languages, educator, grammas and dictionaries. William Carey died on June 9, 1834, in Frederiksnagar, now called Shrirampur, India. Carey did what he did to serve the Lord as a missionary, however, the scrutiny about his care for his wife family was in the spotlight as lesson to be able to balance between family affairs and mission work.

Billy Graham – Billy Graham was born November 7, 1918, Charlotte, North Carolina in his family's dairy farm. Billy's life began to take shape when the Presbyterian raised the farm-boy and he committed his life to

---

[77] Ibid.

[78] Ibid.

Christ when he was 16 years old. After completing his High School, Billy Graham was admitted at Bob Jones College, which was a fundamentalist College. Billy had committed his life to Jesus Christ at a tent of revival and felt the fire burning in his heart for the Lord. He said that he had received Christ, "just as I am" and he was slowly growing to be a disciple of Christ. He then transferred later to Florida Bible Institute in Tampa. "There, he practiced sermonizing in a swamp, preaching to birds and alligators before tryouts with small churches. He still wasn't convinced he should be a preacher until a soul-searching, late-night ramble on a golf course,"[79] Billy was enrolled at Wheaton College in Illinois where he met his soulmate, Ruth Bell, and got married in 1942. Billy had planned to be an army chaplain but he fell ill and he recovered when the II World War was almost over.

After he missed his desire to be an army chaplain because of his illness, "Instead, he took a job organizing meetings in the U.S. and Europe with Youth for Christ, a group he helped found. He stood out for his loud ties and suits, and his rapid delivery and swinging arms won him the nickname "the Preaching Windmill." A 1949 Los Angeles revival turned Graham into evangelism's rising star."[80] Billy Graham's huge crusades across U.S. in New York in particular and Europe, especially in England, put him into the international stage as a televangelist of the world. "His 12-week London campaign in 1954 defied expectations, drawing more than 2 million people and the respect of the British, many of whom had derided him before his arrival as little more than a slick salesman. Three years later, he held a crusade in New York's Madison Square Garden that was so popular it was extended from six to 16 weeks, capped off with a rally in Times Square that packed Broadway with more than 100,000 people."[81] Billy Graham found himself trending on social justice arena where both the liberals and conservative were pointing fingers at him.

---

[79] https://www.americamagazine.org/politics-society/2018/02/21/rev-billy-graham-known-americas-pastor-dies-99?gclid=Cj0KCQjw8p2MBhCiARIsADDUFVH3-B7R8BMHNv hAtuhOjnmsp6p7E_CxHSHzm1eAYAAsQ1ONyUZEeIaAtQFEALw_wcB, (Accesses November 11, 2021).

[80] Ibid.

[81] Ibid.

At first, it was not clear where Billy was standing in terms of social justice but eventually, he made a decision to follow his convictions. "As the civil rights movement took shape, Graham was no social activist and never joined marches, which led prominent Christians such as theologian Reinhold Niebuhr to condemn him as too moderate. Still, Graham ended racially segregated seating at his Southern crusades in 1953, a year before the Supreme Court's school integration ruling, and long refused to visit South Africa while its white regime insisted on racially segregated meetings."[82]

Billy Graham reported that he regretted of not getting actively involved in campaign against racial injustice, especially the Selma, Alabama march led by Martin Luther King Jr. He once said, "Evangelicals can't be closely identified with any particular party or person. We have to stand in the middle, to preach to all the people, right and left," Graham said in 1981, according to Time magazine. "I haven't been faithful to my own advice in the past. I will in the future."[83] Billy Graham's relationships with U.S.A. became iconic and a source of pride as he became the most popular and famous religious leader in America and in the world. Billy Graham was always on the road, married to both Ruth and the Gospel, leaving Ruth with five children: Franklin, Virginia ("Gigi"), Anne, Ruth and Nelson ("Ned").

Mother Teresa – "Nun and missionary Mother Teresa, known in the Catholic church as Saint Teresa of Calcutta, devoted her life to caring for the sick and poor. Born in Macedonia to parents of Albanian-descent and having taught in India for 17 years, Mother Teresa experienced her "call within a call" in 1946. Her order established a hospice; centers for the blind, aged and disabled; and a leper colony."[84] Mother Teresa was born on August 26, 1910, in the Capital Skopje, Macedonia. The next day, Teresa was baptized and she was given a name, Agnes Gonxha Bojaxhiu.

Mother Teresa, was born in the family of devout Catholics and her parents were Nikola and Dranafile Bojaxhiu, were of Albanian descent.

---

[82] Ibid.

[83] Ibid.

[84] https://www.biography.com/religious-figure/mother-teresa, (Accessed January 8, 2022).

Her father was a constructor and a medicine trader and he was involved in the local catholic church as well as in politics, advocating for Albanian's independence. After the death of her father, Agnes became so committed and close to her mother, Dranafile Bojaxhiu, who instilled into her charity. Dranafile was wealthy and she intentionally, invited city's destitute to join the family for meals. "Agnes attended a convent-run primary school and then a state-run secondary school. As a girl, she sang in the local Sacred Heart choir and was often asked to sing solos. The congregation made an annual pilgrimage to the Church of the Black Madonna in Letnice, and it was on one such trip at the age of 12 that she first felt a calling to religious life."[85] In 1928, Agnes enlisted as nun at the age of 18 years old and travelled to Ireland to join the sisters of Loreto in Dublin and took the name, Mary Teresa in Ireland.

Sister Mary Teresa journeyed to India in 1931 and while she was there, she made her Professional Vows. Thereafter, Mary Teresa was commissioned to Calcutta and she was assigned to teach at Saint Mary's High School for Girls. "Sister Teresa learned to speak both Bengali and Hindi fluently as she taught geography and history and dedicated herself to alleviating the girls' poverty through education."[86] Sister Mary Teresa continued to serve as school Principal and at the same devoted her life to charity embracing those who were destitute and disadvantaged.

According to records, Teresa received another "Call within a Call," on September 10, 1946 in which Teresa narrates how Christ spoke to her strongly to leave teaching and to serve the city's 'poorest and sickest.' However, to shift from teaching and concentrate on her new call, it was another process she had endure. "Since Mother Teresa had taken a vow of obedience, she could not leave her convent without official permission. After nearly a year and a half of lobbying, in January 1948 she finally received approval to pursue this new calling."[87] It took her a year to be approved to pursue her new calling in January 1948 and she started to concentrate and serving the city's poor. Mother Teresa started an open-air school and she started a home of dying destitute. Mother Teresa founded a

---

[85] Ibid.

[86] Ibid.

[87] Ibid.

new congregation, Missionaries of Charity, in 1950. Most of the members were former teachers and students from St. Mary Saints School.

Mother Teresa expanded her charity ministry as donations poured across the globe and founded charities across the world. "As the ranks of her congregation swelled and donations poured in from around India and across the globe, the scope of Mother Teresa's charitable activities expanded exponentially. Over the course of the 1950s and 1960s, she established a leper colony, an orphanage, a nursing home, a family clinic and a string of mobile health clinics."[88] Mother Teresa received numerous awards for her outstanding charities that she established and founded. She is one of the most famous women in charity fraternity. "In February 1965, Pope Paul VI bestowed the Decree of Praise upon the Missionaries of Charity, which prompted Mother Teresa to begin expanding internationally. By the time of her death in 1997, the Missionaries of Charity numbered more than 4,000—in addition to thousands more lay volunteers—with 610 foundations in 123 countries around the world."[89] With a flowery legacy of Mother Teresa which has been accredited to her, she also received scathing criticisms for her stands on certain ethical and religious beliefs. Mother Teresa publicly advocated to a "No" vote the Irish referendum to end the country's ban on divorce and remarriage.

Mother Teresa lived for others, especially, the poor, the disadvantaged, the unprivileged, the destitute, the voiceless, the abused, and the sick. She lived to help and assisted human beings who are looked down upon. Mother Teresa, lived a life of humility and scorn yet she changed the world with her heart, service, care and love for humanity.

George Whitefield

George Whitefield was one of the principled figures in the Great Awakening of the early 1740s. The Great Awakening was a watershed event in the life of the American people. Before it was over, it had swept the colonies of the Eastern seaboard, transforming the social and religious life of the land. Whitefield is called the Great Itinerant. He was an associate of John Wesley in England in a very dark time for the church in England. Albert

---

[88] Ibid.

[89] Ibid.

Belden writes: "If we are inclined on occasion to be depressed with the state of the Christian churches in our time, it may be of some encouragement to us to reflect that they are not nearly so sunken in depths of apathy and shame as was the church of the eighteenth century. That century was in many features both the 50Monica Furlong, Puritan's Progress (New York: Coward, McCann & Geoghegan, 1975), 13. 51 Kenneth Dix, John Bunyan Puritan Pastor (Rushden Northamptonshire: The Fauconberg Press, 1979), 5. 41 worst and the best in our history."52 George Whitefield was a man of his time, preaching in the open air and his voice was described as loud as a loud speaker. Whitefield expressed his zeal, convictions as follows:

> The doctrines of election, and free justification in Christ Jesus are daily more and more pressed upon my heart. They fill my soul with a holy fire and afford me great confidence in God my salvation. Put them in mind of the freeness and eternity of God's electing love…Press them to believe on Him immediately … Speak every time, my dear brother, as if it was your last…[90]

Whitefield influenced the church and shaped it according to the Scriptures in the 18th century He is highly respected in Reformed and evangelical churches. He preached the "True Gospel". He was a Calvinist in doctrine and Puritan in preaching. His preaching and teaching brought about the Great Revival in America, working together with others. The evangelicalism spread rapidly and sunk its roots in the churches. The message of George Whitefield, has been summarized this way:

> He believed that the unchanging gospel is 'the power of God for all sorts of sinners (Rom. 1:16, KJV). What was Whitefield's message? The doctrines known as Calvinism: the depravity of sinners and the freeness of God's grace; he rejoiced in the substitutionary atonement of Christ for God's elect; he proclaimed that all those for whom Christ died will persevere to the end of their lives and will then

---

[90] Arnold A. Dallimore, *George Whitefield Vol. I.* (Edinburgh: Banner of Truth Trust, 1989), 409.

be glorified in heaven. Where did he learn these truths? 'My doctrines I had from Jesus Christ and His apostles; I was taught them of God', he wrote, and added two years later, 'I embrace the Calvinistic scheme, not because Calvin, but Jesus Christ, has taught it to me'. Whitefield, the convinced Calvinist, preached the gospel earnestly and persuasively urging and commanding sinners to go to Jesus Christ for salvation.[91]

Numerous sermons, public letters and journals were published during his lifetime and all affirm the integrity of George Whitefield as a Reformed, evangelist preacher.

John Cavin

Prominent figures in church history shaped the doctrines of the church of all ages. I will give more biographical information about John Calvin because he played a pivotal role as a Reformer and shaped the church in Geneva which became a model for the church. The Reformation did not start with John Calvin but he was one of the most influential Reformers. He taught and defended the sound doctrines of the church against heretics who wanted to pervert the Scripture to their own interpretations and understanding. His teachings and contributions to the church are an example of the great commitment to Scripture the Reformers had in defending and shaping church doctrines. Henry Meeter summarizes John Calvin status and his position,

> John Calvin was born July 10, 1509. While Luther and Zwingli were contemporaries, Calvin belonged to the second generation of Reformers. At the time Luther posted 95 theses on the castle gate at Wittenberg on October 31, 1517, Calvin was only nine years old. In a sense, therefore, Calvin rested on the shoulders of the other two great reformers, but he nevertheless deserves a place next to them and is usually numbered as one of

---

[91] Colin Thompson, "*Revival Newsline*: The Reformation and Revival Fellowship," Journal of Revival Newsline, (Spring 2005): 569.

three great Protestant Reformers. The reason for this is that Calvin was the great organizer and systematizer of the ideas of the Reformation.[92]

John Calvin's father wanted him to be a priest; hence he encouraged him to go for priesthood between 1520 or in 1521. Joel Beeke says,

> About five years later, Calvin's father sent his son to Orleans to study law. This sudden, dramatic change of professions for young Calvin is noteworthy also for two reasons. First, Calvin's legal training fostered in him qualities of mind, clarity, precision, and caution that later served him well as Bible commentator and theologian. Second, the University of Orleans was where Calvin first came into contact with Reformation truth.[93]

John Calvin first published his Institutes when he was twenty-six years old. John Calvin's theology has been embraced by many churches and has influenced many people to live and to serve the Lord according to the holy word of God. Joel Beeke asserts, "What a gift the church has in Calvin! Whether discussing economics, politics, ethics, theology, ecclesiology or domestic relation, I know of no man who helps the 21st century church more than John Calvin." He stood out in the Reformation period and he is a true example of a Reformed 41 Joel R. Beeke, "The Soul of Life": The Piety of John Calvin (Grand Rapids: Reformation Heritage Books, 2009), 2. 42Albert Hyma, The Life of John Calvin (Grand Rapids: WM. B. Eerdmans, 1943), 27. 43 Joel Beeke, "Calvin for the 21st t Puritan Reformed Conference" Grand Rapids, August 27-29, 2009. 38 and experiential preacher. His doctrines shaped the church in Geneva and continue even today in the church.

---

[92] Henry Meeter, The Life of John Calvin (Grand Rapids: Calvin College, 1947), 3.

[93] Joel R. Beeke, "The Soul of Life": The Piety of John Calvin (Grand Rapids: Reformation Heritage Books, 2009), 2.

St. Augustine of Hippo

When St. Augustine began writing "On Christian Teaching" in the mid-390s, he had begun on detailed exposition of Genesis, Psalms and Paul's letters to the Romans and Galatians, so to speak. He wanted the readers of the Scriptures to be their own interpreters. Green asserts, "There are two things on which all interpretation of scripture depends: the process of discovering what we need to learn, and the process of presenting what we have learned."[94] He states that all teaching is teaching of either things or signs.

Augustine declared that there are things to be enjoyed, some which are to be used. He said that those things to be enjoyed make us happy and those which are to be used assist us and give us boost as we press on to our happiness. He clarifies his point that the things that are to be enjoyed are the Father and the Son and the Holy Spirit and the Trinity that consists of them as found in (Romans 11:36, KJV). There is the Father and the Son and the Holy Spirit, each of these is God, and all of them together are one God; each of these is a full substance and all together one substance. The Father is neither the Son nor the Holy Spirit, the Son is neither the Father nor the Holy Spirit, and the Holy Spirit is neither the Father nor the Son.

He makes a comparative analysis of medical care the way to health is through medical care; God's care has taken it upon itself to heal and restore sinners by the same methods. So, for the treatment of human beings God's wisdom in itself both doctor and medicine offered itself in a similar way."[95] Human beings fell through pride; God used humility to heal them. We were deceived by the wisdom of the serpent; we are freed by the foolishness of God. It was called wisdom yet it was foolishness to those who despised God, so-called foolishness is wisdom to those who overcome the devil. He says that we made bad use of immortality, and so we died; Christ made good use of mortality, and so we live. The belief in the Lord's resurrection from the dead and his ascent into heaven reinforces our faith with great hope.

We ourselves who enjoy and use other things are things. A human

---

[94] R.P. H. Green, St. Augustine on Christian Teaching, (Oxford: Oxford University Press, 1997), 8.

[95] Ibid., 14.

being is a major kind of thing, being made in the image and likeness of God' (Gen.1:26-27, KJV) not by virtue of having a mortal body but by virtue of having a rational soul and thus a higher status than animals. The question is can human beings enjoy one another or use one other or both? The Bible is clear in that we have to love one another (John13:34; 15:12, 17, KJV). All people should be loved equally. When you enjoy a human being in God, you are enjoying God rather than human being. Paul said to Philemon: "So, brother, I shall enjoy you in the Lord (Philem. 20, KJV). Anyone who thinks he has understood the divine scriptures or any part of them but cannot understand the double love of God and neighbor has not yet succeeded in understanding them.

They are two signs, the natural signs and the given signs. Natural signs are those which without wish or any urge signify cause of something besides themselves, for example, smoke which signifies fire, the footprint of a passing animal. Spoken words cease to exist as soon as they come into contact with the air. It is imperative to be moved by God towards learning His will, what He instruct us to seek or avoid. This fear will inspire reflection about our mortality and future death. Through holiness and not to contradict Holy Scripture and believe that what is written is better and truer than any insights than that we can gain by our own efforts. After the two stages of fear and holiness comes the third stage, that of the knowledge.

He continues to point out that it is vital that the reader first learns from the Scriptures that he is entangled in a love of this present age and that he falls short of loving God and his neighbor to the extent that the Scriptures prescribes. For this knowledge makes someone remorseful but not boastful. In that case, it will bring him to the fourth stage that of fortitude, which hungers for righteousness (Matt. 5:6, KJV). The fifth stage is compassion and then he rises to the sixth stage which is to love his enemy. Those who fear God and are made docile by the holiness of seek God's will. Knowledge of the Bible or Scriptures is the most fundamental things. There are two reasons why written texts fail to be understood: their meaning may be veiled either by unknown signs or by ambiguous signs. Sign are either literal or metaphorical. They are literal when they are used to signify the things for which they were invented for. They are metaphorical when the actual things which are signified by the particular.

Christian freedom has liberated those whom it found enslaved to useful signs. Someone who attends to and worships a thing which is meaningful but remains unaware of its meaning is a slave to a sign. The analogy goes on saying that the person who attends to or a useful sign, one divinely instituted, and does realize its force and significance, does not worship a thing which is only apparent and transitory but rather the thing to which all such things are to be related. Such a person is spiritual and free. All the deeds contained in the OT are to be interpreted not only literally but also figuratively. We must take great care in trying to understand the expressions whether they are literal or figurative. When we observe that they are figurative, it is easy to study it from different angles, using the rules set out until we come to the conclusion to the true meaning of the text. Examination the differences reveal two forms. One of the examples of the forms is 'lion' which signifies Christ in the passage 'The lion from the tribe of Judah has conquered' (Rev. 5:5, KJV). The 'devil' in the passage 'You enemy the devil walks like a roaring lion, seeking someone to devour' (I Pet. 5:8, KJV). A 'serpent' is used in a good sense in the passage 'be as wise as serpents' (Matt. 10:16, KJV), but in a bad sense in 'serpent seduced Eve by its cunning' (II Cor. 11:3, KJV).

There are other things which signify not just single ideas but, taken individually, two or often more ideas, depending on the context in which they are found. Sometimes one or two meanings are perceived in the same words of Scriptures. The person examining the divine utterances must do his best to arrive at the intension of the writer through whom the Holy Spirit produced that part of Scripture. Knowledge of tropes for the solution of ambiguities in scripture because when a meaning based on the literal interpretation of the words is absurd, we must investigate whether the passage that we cannot understand is perhaps being expressed by means of one or other tropes. This is how most hidden meanings have been discovered. The spiritual Israel is distinguished from fleshly Israel, consisting of a single people, by the novelty of grace, not by nobility of race, and by mentality, not nationality. The interpreter and teacher of the divine Scriptures, the defender of the true faith and vanquisher of error, must communicate what is good and eradicate what is bad.

CHAPTER FOUR
A GLANCE FROM
CONTEMPOR AY LEADERS

BIBLICAL ELDERSHIP AN URGENT CALLS TO
RESTORE BIBLICAL CHURCH LEADERSHIP:
PART ONE: BY ALEXANDER STRAUCH

T he fundamental importance of the Eldership in the church as charged to oversight of the church has been shifted and modified from church ages. Elders of the church are charged to guard and oversee the function and the welfare of the congregations. In the early church in the New Testament, elders played important roles as pastors and overseers of the flock. Strauch points out that eldership slowly was drifted away from the church and it was replaced by the hierarchy of officials. But after centuries of neglect of eldership in the church, the reformers recovered biblical eldership to the rightful place in the church. Strauch stresses that there is a need of language reform because titles such as "clergyman, layman, reverend, priest, bishop, ordained and ministerial convey ideas that are contrary to what Jesus

Christ and His apostles taught."[96] Strauch's argument stresses the biblical eldership which was initiated at the beginning of the church. Apostle Paul appointed elders to pastor the churches he had planted. With the shift of the role of elders throughout the ages, he argues that the church has gone back to the basic. The role of the elders cannot be changed because of the situations and cultural backgrounds. The argument of contextualization does not hold water. Scripture teaches that the church should remain in the instruction of the Word of God not to divert from it or try to find ways to modify for self-gratification, argues Strauch. He argues that the terminologies used in the church today like priests, bishops, clergymen and ministers misrepresent the true nature of apostolic Christianity. He argues that the appropriate titles were "Elders." "The term "elder" conveys positive ideas of maturity, knowledge, experience, wisdom and veneration."[97]

Servant Leadership, according to Strauch is one who serves and has child-like heart and humility. Jesus showed humility by washing the feet of His disciples. The proud have no share in the kingdom of God. What Strauch should point out is the fact that the title cannot make the person proud but the attitude and the character of the person. Title cannot humble a person. One can be an Elder in the church and become very proud of him. The elders lead the church (Tim. 5:17, NIV) and Christ modeled servant leadership. He gives the example of Paul as a humble leader with authority. In shared leadership, Strauch stresses that the best experience of pastoral oversight of the church is when there is a shared ministry with the elders in the local church. Participation in church leadership brings joy and responsibility. Strauch argues that shared leadership brings fulfillment and satisfaction to both the pastor and the elders of the church. Shared leadership was practiced in the early church in the New Testament. Male leadership in which men dominate the leadership of the church has brought controversy about female leadership in the church today. With the influence of the Western society that advocates for equality between the men and women, leadership crisis has invaded the church also as feminist movement is getting its grip in the church. There is dissolution of traditional male-female roles in the church. Strauch argues

---

[96] Alexander Strauch, *Biblical Eldership*, (Littleton: Lewis & Roth Publishers, 1986), ix.

[97] Ibid. 14.

that God created male and female as equal in their being (Gen.2:18, 21-23, NIV). However, their roles and duties are different. God intended men to function as leaders, to govern, protect and to provide for the family. By the same token, He created woman to care, support and nurture the family. Their roles differ because of their biological, psychological and social make up. They are both biblical and theological support for their roles.

Pastoral Leadership is shepherd-sheep relationship is the spiritual care of God's flock. Elders are God's stewards. Shepherd demands accountability and responsibility for the flock, to feed, protect, lead and teach the flock. Paul points out in turn, it is the obligation of the church to submit, honor and to love the elders because of their roles in the church. Strauch points out that part of the loving and honoring the elders of the church is by financial support, protection and prayer. Elders in the OT in Israel provide us with valuable background for the NT study of elders. In Israel, both the religious and secular societies were ruled by elders. They are no specific qualifications, appointments and organization of the elders. Strauch teaches that in Egypt as slaves, Israel was governed by a council of elders as leaders and people's representatives. He points out the failure of the elders in Israel when they took the Ark of the Covenant to be exposed to their enemies, the Philistines because they were being defeated. As a result, it was captured. The second failure of the elders was when they demanded to have a king like the heathen nations around them. God gave them Saul who became the worst king of Israel. It shows that the elders make big mistakes also.

Strauch highlights that there is a debate about the origin of the elders in the New Testament churches. Some scholars argue that the early church borrowed the concepts of elders from the synagogue. Surprisingly, in his nine letters, Paul does not mention "elders" but in Acts, I Timothy and Titus it shows that Paul appointed elders. The function of the council of elders was the administration of the church, shepherding, financial responsibility and accountability, praying and laying of hands to the sick and those taking positions in the church.

One of the Apostles, John, the Elder, addresses the issue of eldership in second John and the designation of *ho presbyteros* refers to John the son of Zebedee, one of the twelve disciples. It is believed that John wrote the epistles when he was very old. Paul also used the same word to refer to an old man. In the book of Revelation, John refers to the 24 elders in his vision of heaven in the thrones around God's thrones. The title, Elders in Israel was regarded as the highest council of heaven next to God. Strauch in this book argues strongly that eldership is a biblical title that need to be kept by the church be held, highly than other titles that have featured during the centuries of church grown. His arguments hold water but the titles of the rulers of the church do not change the character, attitudes and moral of individuals. It is not the title but the integrity, the responsibility, the character and righteousness of those who lead the church which matters.

SERVANTS OF SERVANTS: A BIBLICAL THEOLOGY OF LEADERSHIP BY DON HOWELL JR.

Howell spells out the importance of the understanding that those who anticipate to lead, they should do in accordance to God's and biblical practice of leadership on the expressed heart of God. He gives the definition of Biblical leadership, "Biblical leadership is taking the initiative to influence people to grow in holiness and to passionately promote the extension of God's kingdom in the world."[98] He elucidates of his definition of leadership that it is proactive, purposive and comprehensive. In proactive, he contends that leadership involves the initiative to influence others. In purposive, he explains that the biblical leadership focuses on helping both individuals and the whole church to grow in godliness and to fear God. Comprehensively, Howell asserts that leadership can be formal and informal, secular and vocational ministry context because it impacts character and conduct.

The great leaders of the OT are commonly designated "servants of the Lord." Moses and David represent servant-leadership ideals. They stand out among others because of their emphasis and reference to the Scriptures in their leadership. They had a passion for God's glory and concern for the spiritual welfare of the covenant nation and because they prefigured the Greta Prophet (Deut. 18:15-18, NKJV) and the King (2 Sam. 7:16; Isa. 11:6, NKJV). In the NT, the Greeks placed great value on personal

---

[98] Don N. Howell, *Servants of Servant: A Biblical Theology of Leadership*, (Eugene: Wipf & Stock Publishers, 2003), 3.

autonomy which was freedom from subjection to the will of someone outside oneself like in the OT in which slavery was accounted for. Plato, Aristotle, the stoic philosophers Epictetus and Philo all advocated for self-determination which is the heart of the meaningful existence. They castigated that to be subject to the will of another is to be stripped of one's dignity and it is a condition that is contemptible. Jesus is the model servant and of leadership. In the Old Testament, Joseph is one of the characters of leaders who were refined through hardship and he demonstrated servant leadership in Egypt. His character, integrity, humility, discernment, covenant keeper, proved that he was a servant of the Lord who used biblical principles to overcome all the odds against him.

Moses had a character and feared the Lord and was said to be the humblest man in the world. He persevered, was patient and was an advocate for stubborn people. His confrontation, obedience, prayerfulness, steadfastness in crisis, wisdom, mediatory role between God and the Israelites, the lawgiver, intercessor, guardian of holiness and preparing his successor proved biblical leadership skills. Howell continues to talk about the biblical leadership demonstrated by the servants of the Lord. Joshua, a courageous successor of Moses was man of faith and courage, careful planner, military commander and spiritual warrior, administrator and covenant keeper proved that he was indeed, a courageous leader. Deborah, a woman for the times, stood as a prophetess and judge for the nations. She was the mobilizer of Israel's forces and a great singer in celebration of the Lord's deliverance of Israel from the oppressive hand of the Canaanites. Gideon who had divine power in human weakness was a mighty warrior of God who depended on as God's chief Commander of the army of Israel. Samson, who had a special identity and godly heritage, deliverer of the Israelites from oppression and fear of the Philistines was a good example of a mighty man of God although he had a tragic fall. However, at the end of his life, he is characterized by a humble heart of repentance then the recovery of a lost identity.

Howell continues to give good examples of the biblical leadership that proved to be a model for leadership. Samuel, had a heritage of a godly mother, protection in a corrupt environment and who listened to God and understood the message. He was a reformer, intercessor and judge. Samuel had courage to rebuke and remove corrupt people without fear. He was the partaker of the Lord's grief and herald of a new beginning. David, a man after God's heart, he was a Spirit-inspired musician, a humble servant, defeater of Goliath, did not want to touch the anointed of God by force or by spear but waited for his time. He experienced God's faithfulness to His promises. He was a perpetual sinner but he quickly turned to God for help. He experienced the restoration of God's blessings and fellowship, ruling in righteousness and fear. Solomon, when he took over as the king, he asked God for wisdom to rule Israel. He had grave responsibilities, he was a favored son, sought justice for those who were threatened by the kingdom, had pursuit of wisdom and discernment and also applied wisdom. He was the richest and wealthiest man in the world. He was a temple builder, worshipped a majestic Lord and he accumulated wealth, debt, women, and pleasures of flesh which led to apostasy. He disobeyed to follow and to keep the covenant. The leaders who do not follow God's statues will fall away like dust.

Howell, highlights Daniel, as a spiritual leader in a secular setting. He began in exile, with unshaken faith on Jehovah and proved academic excellence in Babylon. He had personal integrity, was an intercessor, undaunted faith and apologist for God's honor. He was a worshipper of God, a spiritual warrior and heir of the kingdom, defied nature over God's protection in the den of the lions. Nehemiah, was a motivator and mobilizer. He experienced broken walls and broken heart. He defied opposition in a godly manner. He implemented justice and compassion. He persevered to complete the project of rebuilding the broken walls. He was a partaker of covenant renewal, and a reformer of community life.

In the New Testament, we encounter biblical leadership in the servants of the Lord. Peter, according to Howell, states that "Peter, a broken rock becomes a foundation stone."[99] Peter was called when he was a fisherman. He became the rock of the church. He experienced a bitter setback. He fell out because of pride and weak character but he was restored and reinstated as a fallen leader. At Pentecost, he was the proclaimer of the risen Christ. He was the apologist of the gospel of grace. He was a servant elder of the church. John the Apostle belonged to the inner circle of intimacy as Jesus' disciple. He was called son of thunder and the disciple whom Jesus loved

---

[99] Ibid., 206.

so dearly. He was an eyewitness of the cross during the crucifixion. He was the elder of the churches and a Gospel and epistle writer. Barnabas, was characterized as a man with a gift of generosity, encourager and power of mentoring. He was a sacrificial giver; he was trusted bridge-builder in suspicious time and a teaching elder in an expanding ministry. He is one of the greatest mentors in the Bible of developing leaders. He was regarded as a resolute defender of the Gospel of grace. He gave a second chance for a failed leader, incredible. He is a good model for leadership development today.

Howell points to Timothy that he had an extraordinary talent and gift of discipleship of new believers. He was trusted by Apostle Paul who mentored him. He was a delegate of the Jerusalem fund. He was also regarded as a loyal son in faith. He was a young pastor of a strategic congregation. To Titus, Howell refers to him as Paul troubleshooter. He was a resolute defender of the gospel. He was very courageous envoy to a troubled church. He was also a leader of a delegation on a sensitive mission to Corinth about following the pledge they committed to contribute to the Jerusalem fund. He was a pastor to a church in unpromising setting in the island of Crete. Paul, was a leader characterized by being authoritative, confrontational, exhortation, accountable, affirmative, sacrificial, and missional, according to Howell. The greatest servant leader of all time is Jesus Christ. He was characterized by willingness to die for the people, humility, supreme sacrifice, forgiving, motivator, encourager, cultural tolerance, prayerfulness, giving, mentoring, leadership, teaching, preaching, interaction with sinners, couching, missionary minded, embracing everyone and a simple King. He was a High Priest, the Great Prophet and an everlasting King.

SHEPHERD'S AFTER MY OWN HEART: PASTORAL TRADITIONS AND LEADERSHIP IN THE BIBLE, TIMOTHY S. LANIAK

Basically, metaphors and similes are more used in the Old Testaments than in the New Testament. The figures of speech convey deeper meanings and are comparative. Laniak contrasts these, "Metaphors are implicitly comparative (e.g., God is my rock, light or shepherd), whereas similes are explicit (e.g., the kingdom of heaven is like…). Synecdoche is the use of a part to represent the whole ('Zion' stands for the Holy Land) or the whole to represent the part ('Zion' stands for the temple in Jerusalem). Metonym is the use of a related object to refer to something. The shepherd's staff, for example, is a metonym for royal office or authority."[100] They play significant roles in conveying hidden meanings. For people to under the Bible clearly, they need to understand the language in metaphors, similes, synecdoche and metonyms.

Shepherds in the ancient world had special roles as well before the dawn of urban civilization. People raised livestock and cattle as their primary form of subsistence. Therefore, metaphors assume cultural context with the lifestyle of the time. Pastoralism existed in patriarchal period. The social and economic significance depended on raising livestock. The ancient societies used pastoral imaginaries to reflect on the notion of people and leadership or rule both divine and human. "Shepherd language was used in stock titles and epithets to define a king's role as just ruler, benevolent provider and/or powerful defende."[101] The use of 'shepherd' in the ancient societies traces back to Moses who started tending the sheep as a shepherd in the desert of Sinai to the time when Israel became a nation under the leadership of Moses. This concept is further reinforced when Israel's ideal king, David, was called from tending the flocks to become the shepherd of God's people, Israel. These two figures are regarded as the prototypes, serving as models for leaders who follow them. However, the two prototypes, were representing the great Shepherd, Jesus Christ, who is the Great Shepherd and the Great King.

The distinction of YHWH as the Great leader of Israel and other gods was characterized by basic principles. The first one was the "presence" of YHWH. Moses declared, "If your presence does not go with us, do not send us up from here. How will anyone know that you are pleased with me and your people unless you go with us? What else will distinguish me and your people from all the other people on the face of the earth?" (Ex. 33:15-16, NIV). The presence of God was the key. The second thing was

---

[100] Timothy S. Laniak, *Shepherds After My Own Heart*, (Downers Grove Intervarsity Press, 2006), 32.

[101] Ibid., 58.

the "protection" of YHWH over the children of Israel. "For the Lord your God moves about in your camp to protect you and to deliver your enemies to you, (Deut. 23:14, NIV). The Lord is the protector of Israel. The third sign of YHWH that He is with Israel was "provision." He is Jehovah Jireh, the provider. God can spread a table in the desert, (Psalm 78:19, NIV). His presence is equated with divine provision. The fourth sign of the presence of God is "guidance." "In your unfailing love you will lead the people you have redeemed. In your strength will guide them to your holy dwelling pasture," (Exod. 15:13, NKJV). YHWH was the pillar of cloud during the day and the pillar of fire during the night to guide and direct the people of Israel in the desert. "YHWH led his flock through the wilderness by the hand of Moses. He then chose another shepherd, David, through whom to guide his people in the land of promise."[102] Everything unfolds to pave the way for the Messiah to come but before that the prophets are sent fourth to deliver the message.

The first prophet who comes with the Davidic Messiah was Isaiah. His prophecies, visions and oracles depicted the coming Messiah from David lineage. "Here is my serv nt, whom I uphold, my chosen one in whom I delight; I will put my Spirit on him and he will bring justice to the nations," (Isa. 42:1, NIV). "Isaiah ends with a grand vision of God's direct reign over his reconstituted community."[103] The second king and the second exodus depict what was prophesied in the Old Testament. Mark is contended to be the first Gospel. Mark's Gospel is a powerful story of the life, the death and the resurrection of Jesus Christ. Matthew was written after Mark. Matthew introduces his readers to 'Jesus the Messiah, the son of David, the son of Abraham.' Luke was written by Luke, a Gentile and a physician, a companion of Paul. "The book of Luke reads like one of the historical books of the Old Testament. He represents the ministry and death of the Lord as a constitution of his canonical 'history of salvation.'"[104] He continues to say that "While Matthew represents more explicit quotes from the New Testament, Luke's account breathes with biblical allusions,

---

[102] Ibid., 115.

[103] Ibid., 130.

[104] Lanaik, 2006,195.

inferences and analogies."[105] The Gospel of John provides the richest example of pastoral imaginary. The book is referred to as "The Book of Glory" because of the passion of Christ during the Passover festivals.

Peter's epistle is heavily rooted in Old Testament language and imaginary. Peter uses the phrases like, 'diaspora', the 'elect', a chosen people', 'a royal priesthood', 'a holy nation', 'a people belonging to God'. "The book of Revelation provides a fitting conclusion to the Bible's shepherd and sheep imaginary. In this apocalyptic letter, rich with animal symbolism, we find a conquering royal royal-Lion-Shepherd who is, ironically, a slain Lamb."[106] The book of Revelation is dated to the end of the first century. During that time there was severe persecution and suffering in churches in Asia Minor.

In conclusion of the book, good shepherding is expressed by decisions and behaviors that benefit the 'flock' with sacrifice and personal cost. "Authority without compassion leads to has authoritarianism. Compassion with authority leads to social chaos. Shepherds must be able to express their leadership in a variety of ways."[107] Leaders are called shepherds, stewards, son, servant, prince and leaders. Leaders will be accountable to all their decisions, behaviors and leadership. The Great Shepherd is Lord Jesus Christ and all leaders should emulate the leadership of Christ in caring, loving, encouraging, entrusting delegating, trusting, and being faithful, trustworthy and visionary, for the glory of God.

HARRIS, MURRAY, SLAVE OF CHRIST: A NEW TESTAMENT METAPHOR FOR TOTAL DEVOTION TO CHRIST.

Murray has written a very comprehensive book that lays out the foundation of those who are called to be slaves of Christ. As much as Murray depicts the relationships between Christ and His followers, he also points out imperative understanding by Christians to realize that they are slaves of Christ when it comes to leadership. He starts by setting up what it

---

[105] Ibid., 195.

[106] Ibid., 235.

[107] Ibid., 248.

really means to be a slave of Christ and then he develops it to the original Greco-Roman world and the New Testament's attitude toward slavery. The topics that he covers are slavery, spiritual freedom, lordship, ownership, and privilege. The slavery metaphor that Murray discusses sets out a good overview of slavery in the early church and the Greco-Roman world and the perception of the term, its connotation and its meaning then and in the context of Christ and His disciples. He has a deep understanding of culture and the Bible and the biblical languages.

"A metaphor is figure of speech that describes one entity or realm of experience in terms borrowed from another. It incorporated features that can be recognized as apt in reference to the entity being described and other features that are clearly inapplicable."[108] The early century understanding of the slave and slavery terminology has to be understood in their context. The connotation and terminology in the New Testament for salve and slavery must be understood according to the culture of the time. The ideas of exclusive ownership by the slave master, total service to the master and total ownership by the master was real and it was the true definition of slave or slavery. It actually meant that the slaves did not have freedom, enforced obedience and subservience. Murray's discussion on slave and slavery probes linguistic, historical, cultural and social contexts that defined slavery in the first century. He draws all the terminologies to the understanding of "slave of Christ." Murray contends, in the twentieth-century, Christianity has replaced these important terminologies, "servant" for "slave", "total surrender" with "commitment" but there is important difference. As a servant give service to someone, but a slave belongs to someone. We commit ourselves to do something, but when we surrender ourselves to someone, we give ourselves up."[109]

Murray seeks to discover how the metaphor of slavery to Christ and God was able to function as a positive soteriological image for early Christians even in the Greco-Roman world. Social institutions carried a different connotation in different contexts, reference to slavery could represent self-basement as well as upward mobility and access to high

---

[108] Harris Murray, *Slave of Christ: A New Testament Metaphor for Total Devotion to Christ*, (Downers Groove: ILL. 2001), 20.

[109] Ibid., 18.

status. In the New Testament passages, there are phrases 'slave (s) of God' (*doulos, douloi, theou*) or 'slave (s) of Christ' (*doulos, douloi Christou*) in which there are found. Murray discusses in details the Jewish slavery, Roman slavery, Greek slavery and the Ancient and modern slavery. In the New Testament slavery, Murray reveals the attitudes towards physical slavery. He discusses slavery and slave owning. A good example of the slave owning is Paul writing a letter to Philemon in which he expresses concerns and love a Christian slave owner should treat their slaves. He discusses slavery and freedom. In this context, he discusses freedom and slavery, freedom from slavery, freedom for slavery and freedom in slavery. He further examines the term in terms of slavery as a yoke, the slave's service to the owner and also slavery for other people.

Murray discusses about the fact of ownership in which he points out that the Bible has a lot about slave ownership with those who were forced into slavery because or those who came into slavery by circumstances and situations. He makes a contrast between being a slave of Christ and being a slave regarded as a property with all human rights being stripped off you. To be a slave of Christ comes with willingness and one is subjected to do the will of Christ, willingly and with freedom. He discusses the ownership of slavery by Christ in which one becomes a servant of Christ and enjoys all the privileges of being a son or a daughter. He discusses the means of being a slave in which, those who own slaves for business or for their own benefits treat the slave as their own property while Christ treats His slave as a son or a daughter who is willing to serve Him without compulsion force. He discusses the marks of ownership. During the Greco-Roman and ancient world, slaves used to have some marks bearing their owner's symbol or seal just like domestic animals. He contrasts the worldly seal or symbol to that of being a slave of Christ in which the Holy Spirit is the seal that Christ has put in the heart of a believer for ownership. The seal is internal for Christ's slave while that of the worldly masters is external, visible for everyone to see and identify. When one is a slave of Christ, He has a good relationship with the slave or a servant. Slavery to Christ has positive implications rather than a negative implications and applications. He exegete (John 15:15; Gal 4:7, NIV), contrasting the limitations of the metaphor. He discusses at length the conditions of slavery to Christ that are set up Biblically with spiritual implications.

In chapter 9, Murray gives four examples in the New Testament about the relationship of a slave of Christ with their service to their master. He discusses Dorcas, Onesiphorus, Priscilla and Aquila who demonstrated their commitment to Christ and used their talents and gifts to work hard to support themselves and the ministry they were engaged in. They were slaves of Christ and also dedicated to help others and to advance the ministry. He states: "A slave is someone whose person and service belong wholly to another... This complete devotion to Christ includes three elements: Humble submission to the person of Christ, unquestioning obedience to the Master's will, and an exclusive preoccupation with pleasing Christ."[110] Jesus Christ is the foundation of Christianity and those who follow Him are His servants and His slaves in obedience to His commands. "Even on my slaves, both men and women, I will pour out my Spirit," (Acts 2:18, NIV). Murray argues from this premise that slaves of Christ do not have a bad connotation and terminology as from Greco-Roman and ancient world but it is more of relational, friendship, obedience and trust on the master who cares and provides for His sons and daughters in Christ. It a fundamental discussion that Murray engages his readers to make them understand that to be a slave of Christ is more celebrated and more honorable because one will be serving the master and Lord of life and the universe.

It is a well written book that is good for teaching and devotions by all leaders who serve in churches, Christian institutions and organizations. It is also very practical for every devotional Christian for inspiration and practical learning.

STETZER ED - CHRISTIAN LEADERSHIP IN TIMES OF CRISIS

Stetzer discusses leadership crisis management that copulates deeper understand in leadership. The major themes in his lessons about Christian leadership in times of crisis first identifying crisis. The understanding the foundation of crisis leadership is the key in identifying crisis as humans are fallen beings and living in a broken world with natural catastrophes

---

[110] Ibid. 21.

and man-made disasters. When crisis strike, it necessitates the activation of leadership. Stetcher points out that leadership starts in the calm before crisis. Preparations for crisis and disasters in advance is the fundamental in terms of leadership. Running crisis diagnosis control, Stetcher argues, is the pivot in crisis management and leadership. The two types of crises are Incident Crisis and Issue crisis. The Incident Crisis include natural disasters such as tornadoes, earthquakes, tsunami that come without warnings and are event based. Issue Crisis include hurricanes that give you time to prepare and warnings are issued.

They are fundamentals about crisis management in which leadership can identify the risk of the crisis and find ways to reduce. Timothy Jason alludes that when crisis hits, in the mind, there is a laboratory in the mind where there is creative thinking, then the work room which is the reactive patterns and then the basement in which survival instincts set in to prepare you to get into survival mode. Dealing a crisis, they are four things to do. Firstly, pause and assess the situation. Secondly, evaluate the damage caused and be sure with the facts. Thirdly, proceed with action plan. Fourthly, recover and restore. As a leader, be diligent in giving out information, influence, instruct and engage with your church, group or organization.

During crisis, communication is very important. Too much communication can confuse your church, group or organization. Make sure you give adequate information which is clear, updated and relevant, thus leading well. People look up to the leaders for their understanding, assurance, clarity, direction and comfort and empathy. Crisis always threatens people's safely, health, relationships, security, protection, trust, credibility and effective communication. People have anxieties, worries, fears, uncertainty, suffering, frustration, depression, during crisis and leadership is expected to engage with the people, effectively and efficient in order to keep in touch with your church, group or organization. It also important for the leaders to be honest and open about the situation. Do not conceal information and the truth of what is happening. Inform them what you know and what you don't know. When you don't know, let people know, communicate, communicate and communicate. It is better to over communicate than to under communicate. If you make mistakes, apologize and acknowledge your mistakes blind spots. People generally like leaders who are honest and are always truthful about themselves and the organization or institution they are leading. Acknowledge the magnitude of the crisis and establish your objectives, goals, vision and practical steps to follow.

Leaders are either born or made. Leaders are different from managers. Leaders either born or are forged. Managers are made created to be custodians of things, materials and people but leaders lead people not things or materials. Leaders earn trust, respect and credibility because of their character, conduct and they are able to communicate their pain, joy, empathy, frustration and their desires about their church or organizations. The leader's tone must match with the emotions. As a leader, you must be able leader to lead from the front in crisis, within, to encourage, to anchor and from behind. Jesus Christ is a good example who led from the front when he was teaching. He would teach from the boat, from Simon Peter's boat (Luke 5:3, NIV). He walked with the people and a woman who had hemorrhage for thirty years touched the helm of his garment and got healed (Mark 5:21-34, NIV). Jesus also led from behind when he sent his disciples across the lake while he remained behind to pray, and then followed them walking on water, (Matt. 14:22-33, NIV). The leader must be visible, available, accessible, open and articulate.

As a leader, know that you are not made of metal but you are a human and in crisis, you may find yourself with fatigue and be physical, emotional and mental drained. Self-awareness, Self-care, soul-care and physical fitness is fundamental into your success. As a leader, you make all decisions during the crisis, and you may loss control with fear, anger, depression, frustration, negative emotions, sadness, and anxiety. For a leader to manage self-care, soul-care and physical fitness, resting and eating well is important, avoid rebuking your subordinates, shifting blame, or self-pity. Have the right perspective, be authentic, discern God's voice, be patient, find a community or people whom you can pour out your heart and let go, and be resilient. As you take care of yourself, take care of your core team physically, spiritually, morally and relationally. Make sure to laugh with your team, care for them, love them, be humorous, meet their needs, allow them to have fun, create a conducive environment to thrive and succeed. Instill hope, optimism, and moral. When they know your presence and your voice is more important than your words you say during the crisis. You have to always provide clarity in your plans and action to minimize confusion.

CHAPTER FIVE
VOLUNTEER LEADERSHIP

There are about five fundamental things that are necessary when enlisting the volunteers to do the task:

1. Volunteers need to be recruited the right ones and in the right way
2. Volunteers need to be placed according to their professions and experiences
3. Volunteers need to be trained and to facilitate skills
4. Volunteers need to be recognized and motivated
5. Volunteers need to be evaluated

It is fundamental for the minister, together with the elders and deacon, to select volunteers through interviews, conversations or seminars to find skilled volunteers who are interested in a particular ministry. Set programs can help people to identify their areas of interests and as means for recruiting volunteers. Another way to identify volunteers is by putting announcement on the notice boards of the church. The use of slides, videos brochure, bulletin and public announcements may attract volunteers to join in the volunteer programs. Job descriptions should be drafted which should include position titles, functions, qualifications, relationships, responsibility and the term of service and committees.

The volunteers need a thorough training because they are ambassadors of the church or organization. Based on their qualifications, experience and gifts, the volunteers must be properly placed. Leaders should receive the basic training in the context of Scripture and the way the ministry functions. "A true theology of volunteers believes that the work of God's kingdom goes on even when the formal or informal programs of the church may seem inadequately staffed. As equippers, we must ensure that God's people have adequate knowledge of Scripture and an adequate unity in Christ so they can grow to maturity."[111] Training volunteers is essential to improving their performance and their sense of accomplishment. Working with volunteers in the church involves four basic principles: motivating, guiding, supporting and supervising them towards their full potential in serving God through the church.

A spiritual gift is a special attribute given by the Holy Spirit to the church of Christ according to God's grace. The three key chapters of spiritual gifts are (Romans 12; I Corinthians 12; and Ephesians 4) NIV). The potential volunteers must at least have the four basic qualifications: Spiritual maturity, leadership skills and experience, teachable and willing to learn with good attitude or cooperative in pursuing the goals and objectives of the organization.

Philosophy of Volunteerism

There are three dimensions of philosophy in volunteerism, Head, Heart and Hands. The Head is when the volunteers are taught the Biblical principles and mandate to get the job done through the work of the Holy Spirit in them. The Heart is the passion, the desire and the love for Christ to continue with His work which He commissioned all the disciples to witness and evangelize the world. The Hand is the practical dimension of volunteerism when they put their hands on the plough. This is the practical engagement of Christians to fulfill the goals of the church and the Great

---

[111] Berkley, *Leadership Handbook of Management and Administration*, (Grand Rapids: Bakers Book Publishers), 1994, 270.

Commission. My philosophy for volunteerism is derived from (Romans 10:13-15, NIV), "For everyone who calls on the name of the Lord will be saved. How, then, can they call on the one they have not believed in? And how can they believe in the one of whom they have not heard? And how can they hear without someone preaching to them? And how can they preach unless they are sent? As it is written, 'How beautiful are the feet of those who bring good news'."

God has prepared the saints before the foundation of the world to "Therefore go and make disciples of all nations, baptizing them in the name of the Father of the Son and of the Holy Spirit, and teaching them to obey everything I have commanded you. And surely, I am with you always, to the very end of the age," (Matt. 28:19-20, NIV). This is the very essence for which every believer has to been called to do. To willingly and freely be used by God for His glory.

Biblical Foundations of Volunteerism

The Biblical and theological foundations for volunteerism are based in the Bible and are in the mind of God. The members of the church who are willing and have committed themselves to accomplish the tasks in the church should be encouraged and recruited to engage into volunteer programs. The church has to put the right people at the right place to accomplish the church's goals. In (Luke 4:18-19, NIV), Jesus points four basic things for the reason he came for; "to preach the gospel to the poor; to heal the broken hearted, to preach deliverance to the captives; recovery of sight to the blind; to set at liberty those who are oppressed; to preach the acceptance year of the Lord." St. Matthew Baptist Church Ministries were founded on these biblical principles and the departments or ministries within the church are coined in Jesus' declarations. Jesus' ministry was holistic, touching spiritual, moral, mental, physical and social part of a human being.

Paul's writings in (Romans 12:6-8, NIV); 1Corinthians 12:7-11, NIV; 28-31, NIV; Ephesians 4:11-13, NIV; and 1 Peter 4:9-10, NIV, indicate that Christians have been blessed with spiritual gifts to serve God in the church. Berkley contends, "Some Christian volunteers work with great freedom and productivity without significant contact with their supervisor;

others feel frustrated and abandoned without frequent interaction with leaders."[112]

Theological

God created human beings with unique gifts and talents which should be discovered, developed and used all for the glory of God. The priesthood has a mandate to proclaim, teach, preach, worship, witness, love and serve. Christ mobilized the 12 disciples first to work with Him and then 72 disciples and then he continued to increase the number as the work demanded. It is in the mind of God to use His willing saints to evangelize the entire glob. Paul's references to the Christians as the members of the body of Christ that died and rose with Christ, it is a growing entity and living with Christ. The church is the organic unity composed of multiple members with different gifts for the edification of the body of Christ (I Cor. 12-14, NIV). The communities of faith and faithful individuals communicate God's Grace willingly and freely. The theological principle is the way the Spirit and the Scriptures indicate that a church's structure is intended to meet contextual conditions and to communicate the Gospel about the risen Christ.

A spiritual gift is a special attribute given by the Holy Spirit to the church of Christ according to God's grace. The three key chapters of spiritual gifts are (Romans 12, I Corinthians 12, and Ephesians 4 NIV. The 27 spiritual gifts are prophecy, service, exhortation, teaching, giving, mercy, wisdom, knowledge, faith, healing, miracles, discerning of spirits, tongues, apostle, interpreting the tongues, helps, administration, evangelist, pastors, celibacy, voluntary poverty, martyrdom, hospitality, missionary, intercession, leadership and exorcism. Every Christian has to discover, develop and use his/her gifts for the glory of God. God has gifted every Christian with a natural talent but the spiritual gifts are reserved exclusively for Christians. Ministry flows from God. We measure success through the Word of God and reliance on the Holy Spirit. We are all participating on what Christ started and continues to do today. It is Christ's own continuing ministry.

---

[112] Ibid., 300

Practical and perpetual program Implementation and strategy

a. Workshops and Updates of information

The programs that have been structured are meant to last and also to be updated and upgraded to meet the contemporary needs of the church and the community. The programs' goals and objectives should be revised at regular intervals so that they can meet the goals and the objectives of the entire church. The ministers, staff and those who contribute to make the programs tick must always make the assessment and the evaluation of the program. The evaluation and the assessment must be done annually in order to keep the program effective, efficient and up to date. The leaders, the teachers and the staff for each program must have further training in order to enhance their skills and keep themselves abreast with new ideas, skills, knowledge, teaching methodologies, books, publications and new information on various topics.

b. Motivation Strategies

Volunteers need motivation in order to see that they are being appreciated by the churches or organizations they serve in terms of their service, time, gifts, money and other resources. Volunteers have needs. When the volunteers have been recruited, trained and placed according their passions, gifts and professions, they need resources to use in order to accomplish the tasks. Poor planning, organization, and evaluation are leadership issues that hinder the ability of a church to staff ministries with volunteers. For volunteers, the common message is giving your money, energy, knowledge, resource and time. The volunteers find fulfillment, accomplishment and experience in their areas of placements and they can use the experience they get in their respective areas of specializations at work or somewhere else. There are two ways to motivate the people: 1) through fear in which people who work with a constant fear of failure are to be motivated. 2) By instilling confident whereby positive motivation in workforce comes when people have confidence in themselves, in the skills they possess and the ability to communicate.

Levin propounds that, "Volunteer recognition is the volunteer's paycheck and it has to be given in a timely manner. A thank you should be given to volunteers as soon as it is appropriate to do so. A handwritten note or a phone call is all that is needed. Recognition to the volunteers must be specific and personalized."[113] Christian volunteers have a desire and want to serve their Lord and the church. The program must have incentives. The standard should be high and the requirements significant also in order to retain the volunteers. The volunteers as well as the programs are needed to be evaluated for improvements. Gangel highlights four important things expected from the volunteer: a. "Willingness to serve, b. Spiritual readiness to serve, c. Preparation for service, d. Faithfulness in service."[114] To demonstrate appreciate to volunteers, the organization should have at least an annual appreciation banquet, personal letters of appreciation, free transportation and payments of traveling expenses, picnics, gifts at Christmas and Thanks Giving Day, etc. The volunteer will feel part of the organization and will desire to continue to serve the organization.

---

[113] Mark Levin, CAE, the Gift of Leadership: How to Relight the Volunteer Spirit in 21st Century, (Columbia: B.A.I. Publishers, 1997), 17.

[114] Gangel, Team Leadership in Christian Ministry, 330.

CHAPTER SIX
THE PROTOTYPE LEADER AND KING

The Threefold Office of Christ

In Old Testament times, Yahweh chose certain individuals and anointed them to serve Him in the offices of prophet, priest and king. James Beeke writes, "Old Testament prophets, priests, and kings were pointed to, and pictured, the work of Christ. Only Jesus Christ, however, was appointed to serve in all three offices. Only Jesus Christ could perform and fulfill all of God's required demands to be a perfect and divine Prophet, Priest, and King."[115] There have been some controversies about Christ holding three offices in His incarnation, especially in liberal schools of thought. However, the evangelical view has proved that the incarnate Christ held the three positions, as this chapter will show.

Christ Jesus was ordained to these offices from eternity. James Beeke writes: "Old Testament prophecy testifies of Him as the great Prophet, Priest, and King who would come. The New Testament confirms that He is the great office-bearer the Word (Prophet), the Lamb (Priest), and

---

[115] James W. Beeke, *Bible Doctrine for Teens and Young Adults* (Grand Rapids: WM. B. Eerdmans, 1988), 11.

the Lord of Lords (King)."[116] The three sorts of persons who used to be anointed under the law-prophets (I Kings 19:16, KJV), priests, (Exo. 27:7, KJV), and kings-all served as types that pointed to Christ. These three offices met in Christ who was anointed for the execution of them all (Isaiah 61:1, KJV). Christ was anointed to preach the good tidings unto the meek, as a prophet; to bind up the brokenhearted as a Priest; and to proclaim liberty as a King. He was not anointed with earthly oil, as the former prophets, the priests, and the kings under the Old Testament dispensation, but with the oil of the Spirit. Each office will be discussed and explained, separately, starting with Christ's office as a prophet. This entire plan was laid before the foundation of the world for the sake of His chosen people. As the Head of the church, Christ had to undertake all three offices, in order to redeem the bride, His church. Christ as the Head of the church is inseparable from His church.

Christ as Prophet

"The LORD thy God will raise up unto thee a prophet from the midst of thee, of thy brethren, like unto me; unto him ye shall hearken" (Deut.18:15, KJV). In the Old Testament, a prophet was ordained and qualified to speak for God unto men. First, he received God's word, then he brought and taught the Word of God to the people. The first person the Bible calls a prophet (in Hebrew, *nabi)* was Abraham (Gen.20:7, KJV). But Old Testament prophecy received its normative form in the life and person of Moses who constituted a standard of comparison for all future prophets. A. Douglas says, "Every feature which characterized the true prophet of Yahweh in the classical tradition of Old Testament prophecy was first found in Moses. He received a specific call from God. The initiative in making a prophet rest with God."[117]

When Christ made Himself known as a teacher and a prophet sent by God, He took upon Himself the office of purifying the temple in order to arouse the Jews to make them more attentive. J. M. Jansen writes, "The

---

[116] Ibid., 11.

[117] Douglas, *The New Bible Dictionary,* 1036.

first narrative is given by John only in the second chapter of his Gospel. But now, towards the end of his course, claiming again for himself the same power, he warns the Jews of the pollutions of the temple, and at the same time points out that a new restoration is at hand. Yet, there is no reason to doubt that he declared himself to be both King and High Priest, who presided over the temple and the worship of God." [118]

The Hebrew word *nava* actually means to experience heat from within and the zeal to be sent out. The Word of God boils in one's spirit and then it sends one to the people with a message from God, like Jeremiah. Christ as the prophet had a burning desire to do the will of God. A prophet in the Old Testament had authority from Yahweh to speak the Word of God without error. Jesus Christ as prophet had that authority and the people marveled at Him when he demonstrated that He had authority and power. Christ spoke as a representative of the Triune God. Christ was the incarnate prophet who was in the beginning and the world was created by him, (John 1:1, KJV). Believers were in Christ in God's decree before the creation of the world.

The prophetical office of Christ is confirmed by both prophecy and fulfillment. Brakel writes: "He was promised as a prophet in Deuteronomy 18:15, KJV, acts 3:22, KJV, confirms that this reference is to Christ; these very words are quoted as relating to Christ. In his sojourn upon earth the Lord presented himself as a prophet."[119] The Lord Jesus conducted himself as a prophet. He was recognized as such by the people. "A great prophet is risen up among us…. which was a prophet mighty in deed and word before God and all the people" (Luke 24:19, KJV). Brakel concludes: "The ministry of the prophets consisted in 1) reception of immediate revelation from God concerning divine mysteries which occurred among prophets with an extraordinary calling; 2) the proclamation and exposition of the word of God; 3) the foretelling of the future events; 4) confirmation of revelation by means of miracles."[120] To confirm that Christ was a prophet: first the prophets received divine mysteries and revelation (Num. 12: 6,

---

[118] John Frederick Jansen, *Calvin's Doctrine of the Work of Christ* (London: James Clark, 1956), 39.

[119] a 'Brakel, *Christian's* 1. 519.

[120] Ibid., 519.

KJV), so Christ Jesus received all these things from God, His Father in that fashion. Secondly, the ministry of the prophets consisted of exposition and proclamation of the Word of God; the Lord Jesus did expound the word and fulfilled it. Thirdly, the prophetic office consisted of foretelling future events. Christ predicted what He would encounter in order to merit salvation for His elect, but also what would church and the world would go through on the Day of Judgment. Fourthly, just as the prophets demonstrated and confirmed their offices by means of miracles, Jesus confirmed the authenticity of his prophetic office by performing miracles (John 7:31, KJV). The prophets performed miracles by the power of Jesus Christ. Brakel notes: "Just as Christ conducted himself in respect to the law, so likewise he proclaimed the gospel as a prophet."[121]

Brakel asserts that Christ administered His prophetical office by His prophets in the Old Testament during his sojourn upon earth (Heb.1:1-2, KJV), and even after the ascension, He continued to administer His prophetical office by means of His apostles, teachers and pastors (Eph. 4:11, KJV). There is a twofold administration of His prophetic office, external and internal. "Christ administers His prophetical office externally by the written and printed Word, and by the Word preached by His servants. Christ administered His prophetic office internally when by His Spirit He illuminates souls by His marvelous light (I Pet. 2:9, KJV). He illuminates the heart to give the light of the knowledge of the glory of God in the face of Jesus Christ (2 Co. 4:6, KJV), enabling them to understand the truth in its essence (Eph. 4:21, KJV), and to have the mind of Christ (I Cor. 2:16, KJV)."[122] As a prophet, Christ teaches with authority. He is all-knowing, almighty, and perfect.

Martin Luther, the great reformer, struggled many years under deep convictions of sin and guilt. As a monk and professor of theology, he studied the writings of many church fathers and the Bible. His mind was continually occupied with religious teachings. However, approximately 1512, as he was studying for his lecture series on the Book of Romans, he read (Romans 1:17, KJV), the last part, "the just shall live by faith." The Holy Spirit enlightened his understanding and this truth of scripture

---

[121] Ibid., 521.

[122] Ibid., 522.

penetrated his heart. Christ, as teaching prophet, spoke to him, showing him that salvation is by faith in the righteousness of Christ, and not in man's merits. The Spirit revealed Christ to Luther. His heart melted. Joy replaced sadness, light dispelled darkness, and peace filled his restless soul.[123]

As a prophet, teaching by his Word and Spirit, Christ performed in the life of Luther that which no human teachers can accomplish.

A prophet spoke with authority from God and people listened to the message. Even the Pharisees marveled at Christ's preaching because he preached with power and authority. Christ spoke on behalf of the Trinity but He was God incarnate. He spoke the truth and He was Truth. The Lord has also made known in His Word what the church of the New Testament would encounter until the end of the world. In one of his lectures, Joel Beeke said, "We need Christ as a prophet, for we are not able to discover the mind and will of God on our own. We need to remember that in the history of redemption, revelation always precedes redemption. Experientially, Jesus as a prophet uncovers our misery by showing us both who God is and who we are. He reveals Himself to be desirable and necessary and precious, too. He teaches us continually so as to work sanctification in our lives."[124]

Christ in his office of prophet was a teacher of doctrine during his earthly ministry. Calvin remarks "The prophets pointed to the great messianic teacher who was to come. They hoped for the full light of understanding only at the coming of the Messiah. Christ as a teacher of the Word of God bears the perfection of the gospel doctrine. God revealed Himself to the Old Testament people Israel; yet this revelation was in the shadows, in partial form through the prophets."[125] God continues to speak by the Holy Spirit through His written word. Christ as prophet continues to teach by the Spirit. He is the representative of Godhead for the redemption of His church as prophet.

---

[123] Beeke, *Bible Doctrine*, 19.

[124] Joel R. Beeke, *"Christology,"* March 19, 2008.

[125] Peterson, *Calvin and the Atonement*, 48.

Christ as Priest

"The Lord hath sworn, and will not repent, Thou art a priest forever after the order of Melchizedek" (Psalm 110:4, KJV). Christ's work as High Priest accomplished the atonement of the elect. The priest (*coheen*), is one who is taken among men ordained for men in things pertaining to God, that he may offer both gifts and sacrifices for sins (Heb.5:1, KJV). James Beeke asserts that, "In the Old Testament, a priest performed three important duties;

a. Sacrifices (or offering) pictured by the priest's offering an animal upon the brazen alter of burnt offerings.
b. Praying (or interceding) portrayed by the priest's offering incense upon the golden alter of incense.
c. Blessing displayed by the priest's returning to bless the people after performing his work."[126]

The Old Testaments prophets predicted that Christ would come as a great High Priest to do His priestly work. The New Testament has confirmed the fulfillment of the prophecies. The Lord Jesus performs the work of sacrificing, praying, and blessing for the elect. He did that work at the cross and He is still doing it for those who come to Him. As James Beeke puts it, "The primary work of a prophet was to serve as God's representative to men to present God before the people. The primary work of a priest was to be man's representative before God to present man before God."[127]

John Calvin confirms the priesthood of Christ by remarking, "Redemption means the reconciliation of God as well as the dominion of God. Therefore, Christ's priestly work is inseparable from His kingly role. Christ has abolished the figures of the law because he fulfills in His

---

[126] Beeke, *Bible Doctrine*, 23.

[127] Ibid., 25.

own person everything that the former priesthood typified. He is priest, victim, and altar."[128]

Christ's priestly office must be understood in the light of Old Testament prediction and New Testament fulfillment. Peterson says, "Yet, it is only in terms of its prediction of its Old Testament background that the uniqueness of Christ's priesthood stands out. In Christ, the priesthood and the ceremonies of the Old Covenant have come to their end."[129] This office is connected to atonement of the elect, the sanctified ones, who compose both the visible and invisible Church.

He is the High Priest because He undertook our infirmities; He became our real representative. By His gracious self-identification with our misery and hopelessness, He inspires us and gives us confidence in His redemptive work. The former priesthood could only typify atonement through animal sacrifice, but Christ is the real sacrifice, by which all our guilt is removed. He is the real Lamb of God whose blood takes away the sin of sinners. The former priests would come with an animal and shed its blood but Christ as the High Priest did not come to the altar with an animal but He Himself became the real sacrifice. He shed his blood to take away the sin of man (Heb. 9:11-13, KJV). When Christ came as high priest of the good things that are already here, He went through the greater and more perfect tabernacle that is not man-made, that is to say, not a part of this creation. He did not enter by means of the blood of goats and calves but He entered the Most Holy Place once for all by His own blood. Christ is the real altar. Christ's sacrifice needs no other ground than his own person. He is the atonement. He is the expiation and propitiation. God's wrath finds its deepest meaning and expression in the measureless sacrifice of His love.

Calvin asserts, "There is a connection between the two things, the sacrifice of the death of Christ, and his continual intercession (Rom. 8:34, KJV). These are the two parts of His priesthood; for, when Christ is called our priest, it is in this sense, that He once made atonement for our sins by His death so that He might reconcile us to God; that now having entered

---

[128] Cited in James Clarke, *Calvin's Doctrine of Work of Christ* (London: Camelot Press, 1956), 93.

[129] Peterson, *Calvin and the Atonement*, 55.

into the sanctuary of heaven, He appears in the presence of the Father in order to obtain grace for us, that we may be heard in His name."[130] Calvin says that Christ's intercession is the guarantee of our salvation and the basis of our confidence in our prayers. The prayer of Christ is a safe harbor, and whoever retreats into it is safe from danger of shipwreck. Calvin says that great benefits to the believers are Christ's ministry of intercession. Christians can enjoy peace of conscience knowing that God has fully accepted them in Christ, and that Christ continuously pleads their case before the Father. As Priest, Christ laid down His life for the elect, those who are redeemed by His blood. He shed His blood for the church.

John Owen writes, "By what means did Jesus Christ undertake the office of an external priest? By the decree, ordination, and will of God his Father, where He yielded voluntarily in obedience; so that concerning this there was a compact between them."[131] In the New Testament the book of Hebrews presents Christ as a sacrifice. B. B. Warfield says, "The biblical doctrine of the sacrifices of Christ finds full recognition in no other construction than that of the established church-doctrine of satisfaction. According to it, our Lord's redeeming work is at its core a true and perfect sacrifice offered to God, of intrinsic value ample for expiation of our guilt, and at the same time is true and perfect righteousness offered to God in fulfillment of the demand of His law."[132]

Christ's perfect sacrifice and satisfaction for sin produced the following wonderful results: He removed the guilt of sin and reconciled God with His people, He fully satisfied both God's justice and His love, enabling rejoicing in all God's attributes to be possible in the salvation of sinners. He secured a complete salvation for all saved sinners delivering from eternal death (hell), securing the right to eternal life (heaven), and restoring full communion with God. He produced a profound admiration and deep love in the hearts of all the saved.[133]

Christ is a priest and his praying work of intercession will continue

---

[130] Ibid., 96.

[131] John Owen, *The Glory of Christ*, Vol. 3 (Edinburgh: Banner of Truth Trust, 2000), 481.

[132] Benjamin Breckinridge Warfield, *The Person and Work of Christ* (Philadelphia: Presbyterian Reformed Publishing, 1950), 368.

[133] Beeke, *Bible Doctrine*, 27.

until the end of the age. His prayers, as the perfect priest, will always be heard by the Father. Joel Beeke said in a lecture, April 29, 2008 in which he summarized three fundamental types of Christs' blessings which Christ bestows upon His people, the elect, "Temporal blessings relate to Christ's special care in His providence. He guards them with the apple of his eye (Deut. 32:10 KJV, John Owen, *The Glory of Christ*, Vol. 3 (Edinburgh: Banner of Truth Trust, 2000, John Owen, *The Glory of Christ*, Vol. 3 (Edinburgh: Banner of Truth Trust, 2000). He keeps and preserves the elect. Spiritual blessings include regeneration, converting and indwelling in their hearts. He enlightens and inspires them. Eternal blessings relates to eternity, when they dwell with God forever in heaven."[134]

The Scriptures authenticate the priestly work of Christ. Christ's office of priesthood was planned by the Godhead before creation for the purpose of the redemption of the church.

Christ as King

The earthly kingdoms are based upon human organization, but Christ's kingdom is based upon power, grace, and glory. The kingly office is the third office of Christ. Christ rules as King, as God, as mediator and as ruler over the kingdom of glory. Brakel writes, "First as God, the Lord Jesus has within Himself all majesty, worthiness, honor, glory and power, even if there were no creatures. He is the King of the church. Other kings have but little power, are fully occupied in protecting themselves and their subjects, and are even conquered by others, but our King is 'the Almighty' (Rev. 1:8, KJV). Other kings die, are deposed, exiled, and cease to be kings. This King, however, 'shall be great, and shall be called the Son of the Highest: and the Lord God shall give unto Him the throne of His father David."[135] God has established Him in His kingdom and has consecrated Him by anointing (Psa. 2:6, KJV). As He did not exalt Himself to be a High Priest, He likewise did not exalt Himself to be King. That Christ was prophesied as the King in the Old Testament is evident from Psalm 2:6,

---

[134] Joel R. Beeke, *"Christology,"* April 29, 2008.

[135] a' Brakel, *Christian's Reasonable Service*, vol. 1, 563.

KJV. Zechariah 9:9, KJV, confirms that. Richard Muller writes, "Christ's kingly office manifest manifests its power over the church as its head and his defense of the church against its enemies. Christ's office represents his post-resurrection work as well as the work of his earthly ministry, death, and resurrection: the threefold office demonstrates the unity of Christ's work."[136]

Christ's reign on earth and in heaven is the kingdom of power. It influences the physical world, governments, laws, institutions and civil society. In the kingdom of grace, His influence is of a spiritual nature, i.e., related to the souls of the people. Christ's church will reign with Him forever without sin, tears, pain, sorrow or death. There will be joy and celebration, worship, praises, singing, and glorifying of Him. Christ as King delivers His elect; He vindicates and preserves them. Christ as King governs and rules His elect righteously. Christ protects them from the attacks of evil and Satan and sin. Christ as the King of the universe, rules the earth. He enthrones and dethrones kings and rulers on earth (Dan. 2:21, KJV).

> If He had not, as our prophet, revealed the way of life and salvation to us, we could never have known it. Since we cannot know salvation apart from Him, it is also true that if He were not our High Priest and had not offered Himself up to obtain redemption for us, we could not have been redeemed by His blood. If we have been redeemed, still we need Him to live for us in the capacity of King, to apply this purchase of His blood to us so that we can have actual, personal benefit by His death. For what He revealed as a Prophet and purchased as a Priest, He applies as a King.[137]

Christ as King rules everything which is on earth and in heaven. He is the King of kings and Lord of lords. He rules over human beings, over both

---

[136] Richard A. Muller, *Christ and the Decree* (Grand Rapids: Baker, 1986), 141.

[137] Andrew Murray and John Flavel, *The Believer's Prophet, Priest and King* (Minneapolis: Bethany House, 1989), 63.

evil and good angels (Heb. 1:6, KJV), and over believers and unbelievers. He rules as the King of the church both in the Old Testament and New Testament. He will come to judge and to rule. His kingdom endures forever. The benefits of Christ's spiritual reign extend to the whole body of Christ's the church and to each believer. There are both temporary and eternal benefits for the believers. He will come to take His bride to be with Him for eternity. The church belongs to Christ, and He will redeem her forever. The office of kingship does not end. He will be the King of the church forever, for that was the purpose of redemption.

James Beeke says, "The work of Jesus Christ in His offices of Prophet, Priest, and King of His church is most rich and valuable. Christ's offices are connected to and interwoven with several other precious truths of Scripture. What a glorious Prophet, Priest, and King Jesus Christ is!"[138] Christ is presented as the Prophet, the High Priest, and the King by both the Old Testament and New Testament. The Old Testament confirmed His coming and his prophetic message and they were fulfilled in the New Testament as the High Priest and perfect sacrifice. The scriptures presented Him as King and Lord who will rule both the earth and heaven. He is the King of power, of grace and of glory. He rules evil and good angels, the elect and unbelievers. Satan is under His control because He holds the keys of Hades and He is the way, the truth, and the life (John 14:6, KJV).

Christ enthrones and dethrones kings according to His will. His Kingdom is for eternity with His elect, and the saints will dwell with Him in heaven forever. The three offices are both earthly and heavenly. Christ is the protector and defender of His church. He is the prophet for the church, the High Priest for the church, and the King of the church and of kings. He will return to take His church to Himself to live with Him eternally.

---

[138] Beeke, *Bible Doctrine*, 45.

CONCLUSION

The rhetorical question posed in this book whether the leaders are born or made has a fundamental quest for the logical hypothesis. The model and styles of leadership presented in the book gives the readers and audience the opportunity to examine each leader in the business community, political bubble and religious sph re by their own standards whether those particular leaders were born or made. The book explores political leaders who had positive influence or negative influence in the eyes of the world. In the context of religious leaders, godly leaders have been mirrored of their characters, conducts and influence to ascertain their leadership skills and piety. In the same vein, a glance of biblical leaders from contemporary leaders is discussed in this book. The book concludes with the discussion of the prototype Leader and King, Jesus Christ who is the ultimate Prophet, ultimate Priest and ultimate King to whom every leader should measure their ability, capability, responsibility, accountability and stewardship with His. His leadership is characterized by forgiveness, love, compassion, empathy and redemption.

BIBLIOGR APHY

Alexander George, *the Handbook of Biblical Personalities*, Greenwich: Seabury Press, 1962.

Alexander Strauch, *Biblical Eldership*, Littleton: Lewis & Roth Publishers, 1986.

Anthony Michael J. and Estep James Jr., *Management Essentials for Christian Ministries*, Nashville: B & C Publishers, 2005.

Beek Joel R. Beeke, "The Soul of Life": The Piety of John Calvin (Grand Rapids: Reformation Heritage Books, 2009.

Bond Stephen B., *Spiritual Authority: God's Way of Growing Leaders*, Joplin: College Publishers, 1995.

Brand Chad, Draper Charles and England Archie, *Holman Illustrated Bible Dictionary*, Nashville: Holman Press, 2003.

Breckinridge Benjamin Warfield, *The Person and Work of Christ*, Philadelphia: Presbyterian Reformed Publishing, 1950.

Bredfeldt Gary, *Great Leader Great Teacher*, Chicago: Moody Publishers, 2006.

Clarke James, *Calvin's Doctrine of Work of Christ*, London: Camelot Press, 1956

Dallimore Arnold A, *George Whitefield Vol.* I Edinburgh: Banner of Truth Trust, 1989.

Don Howell, N. *Servants of Servant: A Biblical Theology of Leadership*, Eugene: Wipf & Stock Publishers, 2003.

Douglas J.D., *New Bible Dictionary*, England: Inter-Varsity Press, 1996.

Frederick John Jansen, *Calvin's Doctrine of the Work of Christ*, London: James Clark, 1956.

James W. Beeke, *Bible Doctrine for Teens and Young Adults*, Grand Rapids: WM. B. Eerdmans

Kouzes James M. and Posner Barry Z., *Leadership Challenge, 3rd*, San Francisco: B Jossey –Bass Publishers, 2003.

=Laniak Timothy S., *Shepherds After My Own Heart*, Downers Grove Intervarsity Press, 2006.

Losch Richard R., *All the People in the Bible*, Grand Rapids: William B. Eerdmans Publishers, 2008.

Meeter Henry, *The Life of John Calvin*, Grand Rapids: Calvin College, 1947.

Metzger Bruce M. and Coogan Michael D., *the Oxford guide to places of the Bible*, Oxford: University Press, 2001.

Muller Richard A., *Christ and the Decree* Grand Rapids: Baker, 1986

Murray Andrew and John Flavel, *The Believer's Prophet, Priest and King* (Minneapolis: Bethany House, 1989.

Murray Harris, Slave of Christ: A New Testament Metaphor for Total Devotion to Christ, Downers Groove: ILL. 2001.

Owen John, *The Glory of Christ*, Vol. 3 (Edinburgh: Banner of Truth Trust, 2000

Tenney Merrill C., *the Zondervan Encyclopedia of the Bible*, Grand Rapids: Zondervan Publishers, 2009.

Thompson Colin, "Revival Newsline: The Reformation and Revival Fellowship," Journal of Revival Newsline, Spring 2005.

Woolfe Lorin, *Leadership Secrets from the Bible*, New York: MJF Books Publishers, 2002.